THE AUTHOR'S GUIDE TO WRITE TEXT THAT SELLS BOOKS

ROB EAGAR

COPYRIGHT

**The Author's Guide to
Write Text That Sells Books**

Published by Wildfire Marketing
www.StartaWildfire.com

Requests to publish work from this book should be sent to:
Rob@StartaWildfire.com

Cover design by Ron Dylnicki

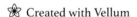 Created with Vellum

CONTENTS

ENDORSEMENTS

"I recommend Rob Eagar to any author looking to take their book campaign to a higher level."

Dr. Gary Chapman - #1 *New York Times* bestselling author of *The Five Love Languages*

~

"I give Rob Eagar my highest recommendation. If you want to increase book sales, make him the first person you hire."

Lysa TerKeurst - 4-time *New York Times* bestselling author

~

"Rob Eagar gets great results and strategically places authors in the right spaces. I'm happy with what Rob did for me, and I highly recommend him."

Dr. John Townsend - *New York Times* bestselling author of *Boundaries*

~

"Rob Eagar provided effective marketing strategy and worked closely with my team to execute new promotional ideas. I highly recommend Rob."

DeVon Franklin - CEO of Franklin Entertainment and *New York Times* bestselling author

～

"Rob revolutionized how I market my novels and connect with readers. His Book Marketing Master Class gave me more fantastic ideas than I knew what to do with."

Dani Pettrey - Bestselling novelist with over 300,000 copies sold

～

"Rob Eagar's expertise helped me develop a new brand and create an exciting new website. It was beyond my expectations and included everything I asked for and more."

Wanda Brunstetter - 6-time *New York Times* bestselling novelist with over 10 million copies sold

～

"Rob Eagar knows how to use words and has fine penmanship. You should really listen to him."

His Mother - English major who taught Rob to speak clearly

MY FREE GIFT FOR YOU

Get three e-books to help jumpstart your book sales for FREE:

Find Readers and Sell Books on a Shoestring Budget

Mastering Book Hooks for Authors

The Ultimate Book Marketing Plan Template for Authors

Join my email newsletter and get these three e-books. Each resource can be downloaded as a file to your computer or added to any e-reader device. You will also receive my weekly e-newsletter packed with free expert marketing advice for authors.

Download these three e-books for free today at:

https://www.startawildfire.com/free-ebooks-ag

PREFACE

If you've written a book, by definition you are considered an "author." Do you know what that title really means? Today, the word "author" means you are one of the bravest souls on the planet. Or, you might be one of the most unrealistic dreamers in our society. Why? Consider the incredible challenge that every modern author must face:

- Over 1,000,000 new books are published every year
- A book has less than a 1% chance of getting stocked on a bookstore shelf
- The average U.S. nonfiction book sells less than 250 copies per year

Source: https://www.bkconnection.com/the-10-awful-truths-about-book-publishing

With statistics like these, it's a wonder anyone decides to write a book. Yet, here you are. You're reading this guide because you're a writer seeking to beat the odds. You believe in yourself even though the numbers say success is nearly impossible. Or, you're just plain crazy, but crazy enough to follow your dreams.

I'm an author, too. Just like you, I chose to make a career out of writing books, even when my friends and family thought I had lost my mind. I entered the publishing world in 2002, before the luxury of fancy technology, such as social media, blogging, or live webcasts. Amazon was still a tiny company that no one thought would survive.

I'm also a maverick. I decided to self-publish my first book before it was cool to be an "indie" author. You could call me one of the original self-publishing success stories. I was just a normal guy who had never written a book, had no fan base, and had no idea what an "author platform" meant. However, I did possess a business education, 10 years of experience working in the corporate world, and a burning desire to share a message that I knew could help people.

Armed with a headstrong determination in the face of my doubters, I tried every possible tactic available to sell my books. I started small, but my persistence and hunger for marketing knowledge paid off. Within a few years, I sold over 13,000 copies on my own, built a nationwide following, and created an email list with over 8,000 subscribers. Public speaking was widely available at the time, so I spoke at over 170 events across North America to more than 35,000 people.

Equally important, I generated a six-figure income that allowed my wife to quit her job and join our business full-time. As my success grew, publishers began to court me with book contracts. I decided to trade-in my indie author hat and become a traditionally-published author. My self-published book was re-released with national distribution where it appeared in bookstores for over 10 years selling another 50,000 copies.

Did I hit any of the major bestseller lists? No, but I achieved something much more difficult. I figured out how to make a great living as an author and help other people through my writing, speaking, and spin-off products.

My success, though, led to an unexpected path. Authors began to seek me out for marketing advice. I was happy to share what I had learned. But, the distress calls from struggling authors became so frequent that I saw there was a need for expert information about how to market books. This problem exists due to the lack of education that publishers provide to authors.

To meet the need for better marketing instruction, I started a consulting practice in 2007 called Wildfire Marketing. Since then, I've consulted with numerous publishers and coached over 450 fiction and non-fiction authors. My client list includes numerous *New York Times* bestsellers, such as Dr. Gary Chapman, Dr. John Townsend, Dr. Harville Hendrix, Lysa TerKeurst, DeVon Franklin, and Wanda Brunstetter. As new technology was developed, such as social media, online advertising, and the growth of Amazon, I studied how to use those digital tools to grow an author's book sales. I know what works and what is a waste of money.

As a consultant, I've helped first-time authors start out on the right foot. Plus, I've helped established authors achieve the highest levels of success. I also published my second book in 2012 with Writer's Digest called *Sell Your Book Like Wildfire*. However, since the publishing industry is constantly changing, I repackaged and self-published all of my marketing expertise into *The Author's Guides* series that you're reading now.

Today, I make a full-time living teaching authors and publishers how to sell more books. It's my dream job and I can't imagine doing anything else. Since I can't be everywhere at once, though, I wrote this book to multiply my efforts and help instruct and encourage as many authors as possible.

The reason why I share my background is because it's imperative that you take advice from someone who has achieved the same goal you seek. As the old adage says, "Never take financial advice from a broke person." Likewise, don't accept book marketing advice from someone who has never written a book or succeeded in selling their work. The publishing industry is filled with the "blind leading the blind." Instead, follow a leader who has gone before you, knows the difference between the landmines and shortcuts, and has the experience to help you navigate a successful path.

This book was written to serve as your personal guide to help you sell more books. In the coming pages, I will dispel a lot of myths and offer a lot of new ideas. However, the information will have no benefit unless you're willing to work at marketing your book. You cannot spend one hour a week on promotional activities and expect to grow. Neither should marketing be limited to only what you do when you're not writing. If you want to reach more readers, marketing should become synonymous with your writing. Engage in both activities throughout the course of your week and month.

I named my consulting practice Wildfire Marketing because I want to help you light a fire under your books, get them in front of more people, create a word-of-mouth wildfire, and enjoy the response of happy readers. When that happens, I hope you'll share your success story with me. That's the kind of tale that I like to read the most!

Rob Eagar

Wildfire Marketing

http://www.RobEagar.com

INTRODUCTION

Which factor do you think plays the biggest role in selling books? Is it technology or language?

Consider the amount of time most authors spend to improve their social media, email, and online advertising efforts. Yet, how much time is spent to improve their marketing copy? Judging by behavior, you would think most authors believe technology is the answer to selling books.

It's true that technology influences every aspect of our lives, including the Internet, social media, computers, Alexa, and e-reader devices. But, concluding that technology rules the day leads to a misconception that can prevent many authors and their books from reaching their full sales potential.

Language drives the book sale, not technology. There is nothing more persuasive at selling books than the words that people see. People do not buy books because computers bombard us with offers to purchase. Readers decide to purchase based upon the word of mouth they hear, the customer reviews they see, and the marketing copy they read. Technology simply delivers those words to a reader's ears and eyes in more ways than before.

Therefore, you can master technology and still fail at selling books. In contrast, if you display powerful language, you can still sell a lot of books without relying on technology. Remember that millions of books were sold before the Internet ever existed.

Amazon may have introduced new technology that revolutionized the publishing industry. But, their computers and servers are just a new means to the same end. The "end" is displaying words that convince readers to buy your book.

Authors are supposed to be the masters of words. Have you learned how to become a master of marketing words? If not, let's fix that problem here and now.

This book will explain how to create the marketing language necessary to promote any kind of book, including fiction and non-fiction. Here's what you will learn in *The Author's Guide to Write Text that Sells Books:*

1. How to write enticing book marketing hooks
2. How to create a compelling book title
3. How to satisfy the reader's burning question, "What's in it for me?"
4. How to write a persuasive book description
5. How to get other people to sing your praises

There's another reason why learning to write persuasive

marketing copy is crucial to your success as an author. Not only does language power the book sale, language is within your complete control. There are so few aspects of marketing within an author's control. For instance, you cannot control the following issues:

- You cannot control if *The Today Show* invites you on TV to be interviewed as a guest.
- You cannot control when your publisher decides to release your book.
- You cannot control whether people decide to leave a positive review online.
- You cannot control if a conference asks you to be a speaker.
- You cannot control Amazon's algorithms.

However, you can always control the marketing text that readers see. And, that's a big advantage – but only if you learn to master the power of promotional words. I wrote this book to help you understand all of the powerful facets of language at your disposal.

There are occasions throughout this book where I provide links to resources and companies that might be helpful. To be clear, I do not receive any commission or revenue from these links. They are just my recommendations for you to explore and decide if it's a good fit for your needs.

Before we begin, here's how I suggest using this book to get the best results:

- Read the entire book first to get the big picture.

- Don't try to do everything at once or you'll wind up overwhelmed.
- Do not compare yourself to other authors or you'll get depressed.
- Decide on one key priority to make your focus for the next 30 – 90 days.
- Experience a quick short-term result and build on that success.
- Don't expect overnight miracles. None of my *New York Times* bestselling clients are overnight successes. Each author worked for years to reach the highest level.

Let's get started. There is a lot of great information that I'm excited to share with you!

1

CREATE AN ATTENTION-GRABBING BOOK HOOK

When I started coaching authors many years ago, I was convinced the most important part of marketing a book was answering the reader's question, "What's in it for me?" Readers want to know the benefits they will receive before investing the time and money to buy it. Sounds plausible, right?

I was wrong.

For example, I taught several authors how to explain the benefits of their books to readers, but their sales barely increased. I was stymied by this problem until a lightbulb moment helped me deduce the answer. People cannot get excited about something that they never see. This revelation revealed that there is something more important than telling readers why a book is worth purchasing. Readers will never see the benefits of your book unless you do something else first:

Get people's attention.

You could write the most provocative marketing text in the history of publishing. But, if you don't get people's attention, no one will see your amazing promotional copy.

Thus, the first step to writing marketing text that sells is learning how to stop people in their tracks and focus their attention on your book.

May I Have Your Attention?

What if you could convince people to buy your book with just one sentence?

What if I told you how to do it in three easy steps? Would you want to learn how? Of course, every author would be curious to know the answer.

That's the power of a hook. And, it just worked on you (ha!)

Imagine the ability to quickly grab people's attention in 30 words or less. Imagine the results if your book's marketing copy had an amazing hook.

A "hook" is a statement or question designed to generate curiosity and compel the reader to want more.

However, creating a book hook is not always an easy task. There is work involved, and it can require several iterations to hone an effective hook that produces results.

Recently, I challenged a group of 15 authors at various experience levels to create a hook for their book and send them to me for review. After examining what they sent, no one passed the test. Every author's attempt was bland, vague, or too wordy. Even the established authors struggled with the exercise.

When I told the group that none of their hooks were effective, some complained that creating a good hook was just too hard. Their tone implied that hooks aren't important enough to warrant the mental struggle. One author even asked me, "I've already sold a lot of books without creating hooks in the past. What's the big deal?"

This author's perspective brings up a valid question, "Is a book hook actually important?" Let's analyze the purpose of a book hook, then you be the judge.

What is a hook supposed to do? One thing only. Get people's attention.

ATTENTION!

In other words, you're not simply creating a hook. You're creating a simple way to get people's attention.

Now, let me ask, "Is getting people's attention important to selling more books?"

Of course. How do you expect to sell something when you can't get a person's attention in the first place?

Attention is everything. It's nearly impossible to sell a book to someone who is distracted, dispassionate, or disinterested.

I've personally experienced this problem. As the author of

several books, I can remember numerous occasions when someone asked me, "So, what's your book about?" In my excitement to respond, I launched into reciting the main points of my manuscript. But, about 30 seconds into my pitch, I could see the other person start to look around the room, or look down at their phone, or even worse, watch their eyes begin to glaze over.

It's a miserable feeling when you lose someone's attention while trying to explain your book.

There's that word again – attention.

On the other hand, think about how much easier it is to sell a product when you have someone's attention. You can feel the enthusiasm, the interest, and the desire to know more.

I don't mean to sound depressing, but consider how many more books you could have sold in the past if you had captured more people's attention?

Without people's interest, your ability to sell books is greatly hindered. It's the reality that every author faces. If you want to sell more books, then get the attention of more people. That's why a hook is important.

Creating a hook might be difficult, but that doesn't mean you should downplay the importance. I know you can do it. How do I know?

Writing a book is one of the most difficult tasks in life. Yet, you found a way to push through the challenge and get the job done. You completed your manuscript. Apply yourself in the same manner and push through the work to develop a great hook.

What if you could increase your book sales just by creating a great book hook?

Do I have your attention?

Good. Let's talk about one more reason why a book hook is central to an author's success.

Word of Mouth is Lazy

Selling books by yourself is hard. Imagine if no one bought your book unless you sold it individually to every reader. That process would be exhausting. But, what if other people helped promote your book for you? Selling a book via word of mouth is much easier. Wouldn't you agree? Every author dreams of readers telling their friends, "Oh my gosh, you have to get this book...it's amazing!"

However, few readers are professional marketers. Instead, they're accountants or managers or teachers or parents or average Joes. These people aren't trained in marketing, nor are they interested in promoting your book as their job.

Most readers, though, are happy to recommend a book if it makes them look good and doesn't require too much effort. Notice that last phrase, "doesn't require too much effort." This reveals a commonly neglected fact about word of mouth:

Word of mouth is lazy.

That's right, word of mouth is laaazzzzyyyyy.

I learned about this concept in a wonderful book called, *Word of Mouth Marketing* by Andy Sernovitz (I highly recommend that you buy a copy... see my word of mouth?) In his book, Andy says:

Word of mouth is lazy. You must help it along if you want it to go anywhere.

Take a moment to digest that quote. Word of mouth is naturally lethargic, which creates a problem for authors. Here's why. Many writers assume after they write a book that other people will love it as much as they do. They expect readers to quickly buy 10 copies and give them all away, or go tell all of their friends to buy books. Word of mouth is going to be easy.

That's not the case. People are busy. People don't always know what to say. People forget to tell others about your book, even when they like it. That's why it's ultimately the author's job to help make word of mouth grow.

How can you help boost more word of mouth? Create a book hook. Here are two reasons why:

1. A book hook gives readers something worth talking about.

Never underestimate the connection between word of mouth and a reader's ego. People like to be the first person to tell their friends about something cool. People are more likely to recommend a book when it makes them look good. People are more likely to mention a book when it spurs interesting conversation. A book hook helps fit that need for something clever to say to others.

2. A book hook trains readers how to spread word of mouth.

A hook can be easily transferred from one person to another. For instance, when your hook convinces someone to buy your book, then your hook also trains that reader what to tell their friends. If they want to spread word of mouth, they can simply repeat your memorable hook to someone else. That makes their life easier.

Word of mouth may be lazy and ego-driven. But, a book hook helps you overcome both of those issues.

How to Create a Book Hook

What if you found out your book was going to be turned into a movie? You'd be thrilled, right? Watching a book come to life on the big screen is every author's dream.

Ironically, visualizing that dream is a great technique to help create a book hook. Imagine your book as a movie. Remove your author hat for a moment and think like a screenwriter.

In Hollywood, a screenwriter's career is based on how well he or she can pitch a movie script starting with a powerful hook. In addition, whenever you see a movie poster or watch a television commercial, there's usually one sentence displayed that is designed to grab your attention.

Screenwriters know that if they're unable to "pitch" their movie in one sentence to a major studio, their idea will usually be rejected. That's because they don't have the hook figured out yet. Movie executives know that a hook is necessary to sell a new movie to the masses. So, a screenwriter must to boil down their entire script into one concise idea that can capture a person's attention.

For example, below are three hooks for popular movies that came from books. Notice how the hook works for the movie concept as well as the original book idea.

What if a man with amnesia has forgotten he's the world's most dangerous assassin?

The Bourne Identity by Robert Ludlum

What if a genetic breakthrough enables dinosaurs to be cloned and roam the Earth again?

Jurassic Park by Michael Crichton

What if a high-end law firm turned out to be a front for the Mafia?

The Firm by John Grisham

Most movies come from books. If a hook can be created for a movie, then a hook can be created for a book. The trick is to look at your book from a screenwriter's point of view.

Writing Hooks for Nonfiction

If you're a nonfiction author, you might be thinking, "Not so fast, Rob. I write nonfiction. Your movie analogy doesn't apply to my genre." Not so fast, my non-fiction friends. I agree that my movie analogy may seem easier to apply to a novel. But, the technique works well for any type of book.

For example, what if you write non-fiction history, education, religion, or self-help? To use the screenwriting technique, imagine your book will be turned into a movie documentary.

I enjoy watching documentaries, especially the "30 for 30" sports documentaries on ESPN. They use a great method to promote their films. When you see a "30 for 30" television commercial, a narrator begins by asking the question:

"What if I told you ___?"

Then, the narrator fills in the blank and completes the question with a provocative statement. Below are several examples:

What if I told you Muhammad Ali was NOT the greatest boxer?

What if I told you history isn't always written by the victors, but by the losers?

What if I told you that sports sometimes IS a matter of life and death?

What if I told you that running a marathon is easy?

For a sample of ESPN's "30 for 30" documentary hooks, watch this YouTube video:

https://www.youtube.com/watch?v=cJRisjTCuGE

Notice how your curiosity is aroused by the question, "What

if I told you ____?" It's a simple technique that's incredibly powerful, even for documentaries.

Here's another approach for non-fiction authors, especially if you write business, self-help, or educational books. Review your manuscript and make a list of the most contrarian teaching points.

Identify the most counterintuitive parts of your instruction or advice. Note where you write something that would make people think, "Wow, I've never heard that before..." or "I've never heard it put that way before."

Contrarian teaching points work well in combination with the "what if I told you" technique. Notice how the following statements fly in the face of accepted beliefs:

What if I told you...anyone can be debt-free in 12 months no matter how much they owe

What if I told you...the secret to closeness is inviting more conflict into your relationship

What if I told you...overcoming harmful habits has nothing to do with your self-control

In many cases, the best ideas for an attention-grabbing hook can be found in the most contrarian or controversial advice within your book.

Likewise, if you've written a memoir or an autobiography, use the same "what if" movie documentary approach. Imagine your book as a dramatic tale playing on the silver screen. How would you make people curious about your story using one question or statement? Below are examples of hooks based on memoirs:

What if a survivalist family forbids their daughter to go to school - yet she earns a Ph.D. from Cambridge University?

Educated by Tara Westover

What if a desperate mother raises her son indoors, hidden from public view, because his birth is considered a local crime?

Born a Crime by Trevor Noah

What if a doctor treating the dying suddenly becomes a patient struggling to live?

When Breathe Becomes Air by Paul Kalanithi

Writing Hooks for Fiction

If you write fiction, you can easily use the screenwriter technique that I just described for non-fiction authors. Imagine your novel as a major motion picture, such as a thriller, a romantic comedy, or a horror film. As mentioned in the previous section, think like a screenwriter and consider how you would pitch your book as a movie to a studio executive in one sentence.

Like most movies, the hook for a novel presents a heroic quest and the conflict that the protagonist will experience along the way. For instance, you can separate key parts of your story into these three questions to help develop a screenwriter's pitch:

1. What makes the main character unique?
2. What type of quest or journey does the main character undertake?
3. What kind of conflict or villain does the main character encounter during the quest?

Below are some examples of how answering these three questions can lead to an interesting hook:

A retired cop. A town in need of justice. Can one man stop a ruthless cartel from killing the innocent?

A poor girl emigrates to America. Against all odds, she completes law school. But, can she take down a deadly human trafficking ring preying on other immigrants?

A neglected daughter. Her desperate search for love. Can a poor maiden win the heart of a rich baron?

Imagine pitching your book as a movie script and use the three screenwriter questions to sum up your story into a pithy sentence or series of short phrases.

Your initial attempts may be difficult. That's normal. When I create hooks for my books or my author clients, I rarely nail the hook on the first try. Do not give up. Worse, don't kid yourself and settle for a bland hook that you know is lackluster.

A bland hook isn't a hook at all. It's just a boring sentence that causes readers to lose interest. Worse, a bland hook causes you to lose precious book sales. Trust me, it's worth the extra time and effort to develop a hook that generates a noticeable reaction from the reader. I've helped several authors increase their conversion rates on Amazon almost overnight simply by developing a better hook.

It doesn't matter what technique you use to create a hook as long as the end result is effective. You can use the screenwriter's 3-question technique. Or, you can also use the "what if I told you" question to help put your brain in the right mindset. Effective hooks make readers want to know how the story in a novel will play out. A sense of curiosity is automatically aroused.

In addition, an effective hook is concise, easy to say, and easy to understand. A long sentence rarely qualifies as a hook, because it requires too much mental energy to keep the reader engaged.

Thus, I always recommend keeping your hook as brief as possible. Fifteen words or less is typically ideal. Brevity matters for three reasons:

1. The more words that you try to cram into one sentence, the harder it becomes for people to read that sentence quickly and fluidly. Good hooks must be easily digestible.

2. Your hook will be used as the attention-grabber for online advertising purchased on Amazon, Facebook, and BookBub, which typically have a short word count limit or tight space restrictions.

3. Most importantly, the longer a hook becomes, the harder it is for readers to share that hook with friends and help spread word of mouth.

Keep your book hook short and concise. Use as few words as needed and avoid going past 25 words.

To make sure you know how to identify powerful hooks, let's look at several fiction and nonfiction examples to understand the goal that you want to achieve.

Examples of Ineffective Hooks

Many of the authors that I coach find it easier to create a book hook by seeing the difference between good and bad examples. Let's start with what NOT to do. Read the following "what if" questions and ask yourself if they grab your attention:

What if you could wake up every day feeling good?

This hook attempt is too vague and generic. You can't tell what makes the book unique.

What if I told you everything you know about love is a lie, but the truth may be more than you can handle?

This hook attempt sounds unrealistic and trite. It feels too much like an infomercial.

What if a teenage girl accidentally time traveled and fell into the body of a rebellious medieval woman who witnessed a murder and fell in love with a nobleman all the while trying to find a way home before she disappears forever?

This hook attempt is so long and confusing that it's hard to maintain attention by the sentence's end.

What if I you could dance your way to a lasting relationship?

This hook attempt is too ambiguous and needs more detail to grab someone's interest.

Use these examples above as clarification about what NOT to do. If your hook attempt is vague or too long, it will just be an attempt – not an actual marketing hook.

Also, avoid using clichés or overly sensational language to cover up a lack of genuine suspense or intrigue. For instance, these clichés don't add value to the hook, such as "like you've never heard before," "you won't believe it," or "the best ever." Empty phrases just water down a hook's attempt into meaningless mush.

Tease, Don't Describe

A common problem for fiction writers is the tendency to describe their story, rather than tease the reader. But, readers aren't necessarily moved by the details of your story. Instead, they are moved by the suspense of not knowing what will happen in your story.

Avoid the desire to describe everything about your story. Trying to cram too many details into your hook will make the sentence too long and hard to follow.

For example, I coached an author whose initial hook attempt for a novel contained 25 words. The problem stemmed for the author trying to include too many descriptive elements, such as the protagonist's age, phase of life, along with the villain that was encountered. You can see the problem below:

What if an aging entrepreneur and a retired Delta Force colonel must break the law in order to save America from a ruthless terrorist attack?

The longer a sentence gets, the less power it contains. When you try to write a hook that contains too many descriptive details, the reader can struggle to stay engaged. Skeptical readers who view your book for the first time aren't interested in processing a bunch of information. They just want to know if your novel seems like an entertaining read. Avoid cramming too many descriptive elements into your hook. Save those details for your book description.

For instance, I showed the author in the example above how to tease the reader by boiling the hook down to the core essence of the story, which only takes 7 words. Notice how the statement below has a lot more punch when the extraneous details are removed:

Breaking the law never seemed so right.

Remember, your hook is NOT the book description or synopsis for your novel. It is merely one sentence designed to make readers want to explore your book description. Most people won't feel interested to read your book description unless you display a hook to pique their curiosity first.

Tease, Don't Teach

Some nonfiction authors struggle to write effective hooks

because they attempt to use the hook as a teaching point. This misstep typically affects academic, religious, or business authors who are too focused on their methodology or curriculum. At times, academic authors can struggle to get out of their own head and view their book from the perspective of an uninitiated reader.

When most people see your book for the first time, it might be via a Facebook ad, an Amazon ad, or the top of the description page on Amazon, Kobo, Apple, or Barnes & Noble.com. In these situations, the average person is apathetic, cynical, or distracted. They don't care about your special teaching methodology, your six steps for success, your proven plan, or your sacred insights. All readers care about is: "What's in it for me?" That's why you need a hook to capture people's attention.

Thus, the purpose of a hook is to tease, not to teach. You can't teach people anything until you have their attention first. For example, the statement below concentrates too much on trying to teach the reader, rather than generate curiosity.

What if loving your spouse requires learning how to implement the three steps of forgiveness?

Readers don't care if you have three steps, five techniques, or 10 magic secrets. That doesn't mean your steps or techniques aren't valuable. The teaching component of your book is important. But, many people won't get interested in your methodology unless you use a hook to gain their interest. For example, you could take the didactic statement above about the "three steps of forgiveness" and turn it into an effective hook in the following manner:

What if love isn't enough to make marriage great?

Now, you've got a hook that grabs people attention. Once a reader's curiosity is aroused, then you can explain how your teaching content will improve their life. Tease first, teach later.

Say More by Saying Less

The power of a hook lies in the ability to tease the reader using as few words as possible. Using the "What if I told you..." technique can be a great way to unleash your creativity and spark ideas that will tease readers. However, using the phrases, "What if I told you" or "What if," to begin your hook can add unnecessary length that steal the thunder from your hook.

Your hook will look and sound more persuasive by using as few words as possible. So, don't be afraid to jettison the "What if" words and display a powerful statement that grabs people's attention.

Here's an example from a nonfiction perspective. The "What if" question below has 21 words. When you display such a long sentence, people can look at all the words and decide to skip over reading it. When people skip over reading your hook, they tend to skip over reading your description. When people tend to skip over reading your description, you tend to lose a lot of book sales. Follow my drift?

What if I told you that anyone could be debt-free in 12 months, no matter how much money you might owe?

When you have a hook attempt that is too long, drop the "what if" part and experiment with turning everything into a short statement. In our example above, the 21-word "what if" question can be shortened into a 12-word statement that packs a potent punch:

Be debt-free in 12 months...no matter how much you owe!

The purpose of a hook is to tease the reader. But, it's hard to tease someone when the sentence is too long to keep the reader's interest.

When in doubt, shorten the word count.

Let's look at numerous ways great hooks can be displayed for fiction and nonfiction books.

Examples of Effective Fiction Book Hooks:

A hook is not a hook unless it teases the reader to know what happens in the story. Notice the provocative power of these hooks for novels:

Beware a calm surface - you never know what lies beneath.

The first man to walk on Mars is sure he'll be the first to die there.

A heartbroken man grieves over his dead girlfriend...until she reappears.

Could you let thousands of strangers die in order to save your family?

What if you could see your life as if you were never born?

Intelligent machines have calculated that the best source of energy...is humans.

Lydia is dead, but they don't know this yet.

Turning a corrupt U.S. Congressman is cheaper than you think. Now, America must pay the price.

Each of these hooks are concise, punchy, and effective. Create a powerful hook and give your story the same treatment that it deserves.

Examples of Effective Nonfiction Book Hooks:

The following nonfiction hooks are persuasive due to their brevity and ability to generate immediate curiosity:

You can train your brain to win.

Rare rainforest land...equal to 31 million football fields...is destroyed every year!

This one secret can take five strokes off of your golf game.

What if you could say no without feeling guilty anymore?

Everyone speaks...but not everyone is heard.

Why get mad or try to get even? Instead, get what you want!

Notice how each hook grabs your attention. You may not agree with the premise, but it's hard to deny the desire to know more. That's the purpose of a hook. Make people curious. Make them wonder. Make them fascinated.

By the way, if you're tight on word count when displaying a book hook, you can drop the "what if" part at the beginning and turn it into a statement. For example:

"*What if I told you four Jamaicans decided to enter the Winter Olympics as a bobsled team...but have never seen snow?*" can be shortened to: "*Four Jamaicans enter the Winter Olympics as a bobsled team...but have never seen snow.*"

"*What if I told you everyone speaks, but not everyone is heard?*" can be shortened to: "*Everyone speaks, but not everyone is heard.*"

In many cases, a concise statement can pack even more promotional punch than a "what if" question.

Now that you know the difference between enticing hooks and bland attempts, the next step is to learn where to use your hook.

Where to Use Your Book Hook

What if I told you that your book hook is useless unless people actually see it?

Once you have a good hook, where do you use it? The answer is: EVERYWHERE.

A book hook only has power if readers see it. That's why a hook should be displayed prominently wherever people view information about your book. Here are four key places to use your hook:

1. Display your hook on the back cover copy

On your physical book cover jacket, feature your book hook as the first sentence on the top of your back cover copy. When people browse at a bookstore, many readers look at the front cover then flip the book over to read the back cover copy. Make your hook the first words people see on the back cover. Use a larger font, bolded text, or a different color to make the words stand out.

Plus, there are some instances where your hook might serve as an effective subtitle. For instance, if you struggle to develop a supportive subtitle, try using your book hook in its place. A great hook doesn't need to be relegated to the back cover. You can also feature the words on the front cover along with the main title.

2. Feature your hook on your book's Amazon page

Amazon is the largest book retailer in the world. Every day, millions of people search, browse, and buy new books. Their website has the power to display your book hook to more readers than anywhere else. But, you must take steps for the hook to be easily viewable. Otherwise, it can appear like any other generic text on the screen.

For instance, make sure your hook is the first sentence featured at the top of your book's product detail page on Amazon. Put the words in bolded text for visual emphasis. In most cases, Amazon only displays an abbreviated paragraph of 30 words or less. Beyond that tiny amount, people have to click on a "Read more" link to access all of a book's promotional copy.

In other words, people won't read the full marketing text if the first paragraph doesn't grab their attention. That's why your hook should be listed first. Fortunately, Amazon allows authors and publishers to use HTML code to make the top section stand out with bolded text and line breaks. For a deeper dive on this topic, read my book, *The Author's Guide to Marketing Books on Amazon.*

3. Amazon, BookBub, and Facebook Ads

If you buy Amazon, BookBub, or Facebook ads to promote your book, these platforms allow you to insert a hook to make the ad more effective. For example, Amazon lets you insert around 30 words of "custom text" as promotional copy for shoppers to see on an ad. Use your hook in that section. Likewise, Facebook and BookBub ads provide a section called "headline text" where you can insert a hook for people to see. If you want your ads to work effectively, you must grab people's attention first. A hook is your secret weapon.

4. Say your book hook out loud

Another way to heighten interest in your book is by saying your hook in conversation with other people. For example, use your book hook in casual discussion with friends, during media interviews, while sitting next to someone on the airplane, whenever you pitch a book idea to an agent or publisher, etc.

A great hook enables you to feel more confident about marketing your book. It can even make you look forward to describing it to other people. You no longer have to fear the question someone might ask, "What is your book about?" Confidently reply by stating your book hook.

There's no bad place to display or recite a great hook. Use it everywhere all the time. People won't tire of seeing it or hearing it. More importantly, a great hook helps your fans spread more word of mouth by knowing exactly what to tell their friends.

Let's recap everything you learned in this chapter into three simple steps. Here's how to create a powerful book hook:

Step 1 - Imagine your book is turned into a movie or a documentary.

Step 2 - Develop a hook using the three-step screenwriter's pitch or employ the "what if I told you" technique. Cut out all extraneous words to make your hook short and punchy.

Step 3 – Display your book hook and use it everywhere.

What if I told you a simple secret that could revolutionize your book sales?

Now you know. It's a *book hook*.

2

DEVELOP A COMPELLING TITLE

You're probably familiar with the old adage, "Never judge a book by its cover." That notion may be true about book covers, but it doesn't apply to book titles. Every day, people judge books by the titles they see or hear.

Compelling titles attract interest and stimulate a purchase, while dull titles cause people's eyes to glaze over and lose interest. Effective titles drive sales by:

- Attracting attention and generating curiosity
- Suggesting how a book's content will entertain or educate the reader
- Hinting at the results or benefits the reader will enjoy from the book

For example, *Million Dollar Consulting* by Alan Weiss is the compelling title of a popular non-fiction business book. The title alone causes entrepreneurs to conjure up thoughts of making a million dollars as a consultant and living a successful lifestyle.

Crazy Rich Asians by Kevin Kwan is the provocative title of a bestselling novel that was turned into a hit movie. The title itself causes people to conjure up thoughts of funny stories about Asian characters with a satirical view of their culture.

If language is the power of the sale, your title acts like fuel to energize the sales process. After 10 years working in the publishing industry, I'm still amazed by the sway that a title can have over thousands of people. One clever word or a few well-connected words can lead people to snap up a book and look forward to reading it.

In contrast, an ineffective title has the opposite effect. Lousy titles hinder book sales by causing these problems:

- Failure to gain the reader's attention
- Confusing readers about the book's content
- Lack of hinting at the benefits or the payoff the reader will experience

So, how do you know the difference between a compelling title and an ineffective title? Is it just a crapshoot? Is it personal preference? Is it flipping a coin or drawing straws?

Let me answer by emphasizing there is no single correct way to create a great title. Anyone who claims otherwise is lying. There are lots of ways to develop effective titles. It's a creative endeavor just like making music or painting fine art.

There is no perfect titling method. There is no perfect word count, although shorter is usually better. There is no perfect title that everybody likes. No matter how many copies you sell, some people will still hate your title.

To be clear, reading this chapter won't make an incredible title magically appear for your next book. Instead, the tips within these pages will help you determine if the titles you develop abide by logical marketing principles that have stood the test of time.

Is it mandatory to create a compelling title in order to sell a lot of books? No, there are plenty of books listed on the *New York Times* bestseller list with boring, vague, and lackluster titles. Those books sold well in spite of a bad title, due either to the strength of the author's celebrity status, a huge marketing budget, or a uniquely amazing manuscript. But, imagine how many more copies would have sold in those cases if the book had an exceptional title.

There are a myriad of factors that influence the success of a book. That's why writing a book sometimes feels like gambling at a casino. There are numerous elements beyond the author's control, such as the publisher's choice of publication date, the competition, the economy, the support from retailers, the current media headlines, etc.

However, there are still a few factors that any author can control. One of these controllable factors is your book title. You ultimately get to decide the words that people see as the name your book. If language can influence how people decide to purchase, then why not make your title as compelling as possible?

I don't want to insult your creativity by telling you how to create a title. But, I do want to guide you through the decision-making process using principles that work in your favor. There are reasons why some titles shine and others flop.

Also, if you happen to suffer from "title block," I'll offer steps you can take to spark new ideas. To aid your creative titling process, I will cover these issues in this chapter:

- Your book title should tease, not teach
- Five questions to ask when evaluating a title
- Never underestimate the reader ego
- The "one-word" title technique

As we explore these concepts, you will see numerous examples of excellent titles. Use them to understand why my recommended principles work and how to help develop better title options for your next book.

Your Book Title Should Tease, Not Teach

Below is a book with two different title options. Which option do you find more appealing?

Book 1

Option A: *Conscious Couplehood*

Option B: *Getting the Love You Want*

. . .

Book 2

Option A: *What Happens When a Cheez-Its and Chocolate Girl Gets Healthy*

Option B: *Made to Crave*

Which title is the better option? The answer is obvious, right? In both cases, Option B is the more appealing title. In fact, both of those titles wound up becoming runaway *New York Times* bestsellers. However, in each situation, the author originally wanted to use Option A. Imagine the apathetic reaction if readers had seen Option A. Neither of those titles make sense.

Authors often fall in love with a title while writing their manuscript. That working title might represent something personal and meaningful to them. But, it may not convey a enticing idea to the uninitiated reader.

I know the two *New York Times* bestselling authors who wrote the books we just examined. When they told me their titling stories, both initially wanted to use Option A as the name for their books. Fortunately, cooler heads prevailed and they went back to the drawing board to develop new options. Today, they're glad they changed their mind and pushed themselves to create Option B. Those titles literally changed their careers by helping each author become a bestseller.

Yet, why did these authors make the original mistake of believing Option A was a good idea? Why was their thinking incorrect? The answer is that they didn't know the ultimate purpose for creating a book title:

The ultimate purpose of a book title is to tease, not to teach.

Never view your title as a teaching tool. Instead, it is a teasing tool. Your title's job is to draw readers to your book, not teach readers what you know. Teasing the reader with your title isn't a manipulative trick. It's a legitimate technique that is necessary to capture people's interest. Without interest, there is no book sale. For example, notice how these titles tease you to want more information about the book.

Examples of Fiction Titles that Tease

The President is Missing

A Killer's Mind

Something in the Water

The Other Woman

The Outsider

The Wife Between Us

The Couple Next Door

City of Endless Night

The Two Kinds of Truth

Left Behind

The Auschwitz Escape

Examples of Non-fiction Titles that Tease

The Truth About Men

The Life-Changing Magic of Tidying Up

Born a Crime

The 7 Habits of Highly Effective People

How to Win Friends and Influence People

The Plant Paradox

The Five Love Languages

Never Split the Difference

How to Change Your Mind

The Immortal Life of Henrietta Lacks

Safe People

Battlefield of the Mind

Hopefully, I've teased your interest to improve your next book title. So, let's look at specific steps you can use develop a captivating title.

4 Questions to Create a Compelling Book Title

As a marketing consultant who's coached over 450 authors, I'm frequently asked, "What's the secret to a captivating book title?" As stated earlier in this chapter, I don't have a secret. Instead, I teach authors how to create titles based on solid marketing principles. Four of these principles can be utilized by examining your title according to the following questions:

Question 1 – Is the title easy to remember a week later?

Develop a title and then walk away for seven days. If you can quickly remember the title after a week, you're on the right track. Great titles allow our brains to embed the phrase in our memory for easy recall. Short titles that are punchy aid the memorizing process. That's why concise titles tend to be more effective. Here are some great examples: *Love Wise; Made to Crave; Diary of a Wimpy Kid*

Question 2 – Does the title create immediate curiosity?

A captivating title should create a reaction within people to want to know more. Ideally, you want a title to make someone think, "I can't wait to read that book!" Notice how these counterintuitive titles create a natural sense of curiosity: *Safe People; 90 Minutes in Heaven; The World is Flat*

Question 3 – Does your title imply value for the reader?

This question applies primarily to non-fiction books. Besides creating curiosity, a title should also imply the promise of something the reader will receive and answer the reader's ultimate question, "What's in it for me?" Effective examples include: *You Are a Badass at Making Money; What to Expect When You're Expecting; The Power of a Positive No*

Question 4 – Does your title help build a series or a brand?

If you intend to create a series of related books, then the title you develop for the first book is vitally important. You want that title to be flexible enough to work in conjunction with the follow-up books. For example, the title of this book is *The Author's Guide to Write Text That Sells Books*. I'll confess that this title may not be overly striking. But, there's a larger purpose at work. My title works well for my ultimate goal of creating a series of books that go together. I needed a base title that can be repeated with the other books in my series, such as *The Author's Guide to Email Marketing* and *The Author's Guide to Marketing Books on Amazon*.

If you plan to build a brand or develop a series, you want a title that can work well for multiple books and any accompanying products, such as workbooks, video courses, speaking seminars, or a trilogy of novels. Some of the most successful book series include *Harry Potter, Chicken Soup for the Soul, The Berenstain Bears, The Lord of the Rings,* and *The Adventures of Sherlock Holmes*. Each of the original books spawned a long-lasting series and created a lucrative career for the authors.

I use these four questions when helping my clients create captivating book titles. However, if you still find yourself stuck, try the following tips to overcome the problem of "title block."

How to Overcome Title Block

Most authors are familiar with the dreaded problem of getting "writer's block." You're ready to write, but a blank computer screen stares back at you and your brain seems empty of fresh ideas. You may fear that your author career is over. Eventually, though, the logjam breaks and you get your writing mojo back.

A similar frustration can occur when developing ideas for a book title. All of your title options seem to feel flat or lack pizzaz. If you struggle with "title block," use these proven techniques I've shared with clients to break out of a creative funk:

Step 1 – If you've written all or a portion of your manuscript, scan the content and make a list of any sentence or phrase that sounds contrarian, counterintuitive, confrontational, or provocative. Put all of those sentences or phrases into a separate list.

Step 2 – Review your list and examine if any of those contrarian phrases spark ideas for a great title.

Step 3 – To help narrow down the best possibilities, apply the following three techniques to your list to help make ideas for a great title stand out:

a. Employ the use of alliteration

Alliteration is the occurrence of the same letter or sound at the beginning of adjacent or closely connected words. For example, *The Money Maker* or *The Secret to Changing Your*

Spouse use alliteration. Notice how using M and M or S and S together give those titles a smooth flow.

b. Start your title with a number

Memorable titles for non-fiction books can be created by adding a number to the beginning, such as *The 5 Love Languages* or *The 7 Habits of Highly Effective People*. If your manuscript content covers a set number of instructional tips, experiment with using that number in the title.

c. Modify a famous adage

Modifying a famous adage that relates to your book's content can also help develop a creative title. For instance, these titles play off of popular sayings in culture, *Beggars Can Be Choosers* and *A Penny Saved Won't Make You Rich*. Instead of "follow the leader," turn the adage around to say *Lead Like a Follower*.

"Title block" typically occurs due to one of three issues:

- lack of diverse ideas
- lack of identifying counterintuitive material within your manuscript
- lack of patience or rushing the creative process.

Overcome these problems by applying your creativity and giving yourself time to mull over several ideas for a few days or weeks. By using the techniques described above, you can create a wide range of good candidates to consider.

However, there is another little-known factor about titles that every author should take into account. This component involves how people feel if seen reading your book in public. The next section explains this unusual psychological effect on the decisions you make about a title.

Never Underestimate the Reader Ego

There is a hidden factor that affects reader behavior towards a book that many authors overlook, which is the reader's ego. In most cases, you are selling books to adults. Even most children's books are selected by adults. But, adults still have egos that harken back to high school when we wanted to feel cool and accepted. Thus, if your title clashes against a reader's ego, you can lose the book sale.

Many people are uncomfortable being seen with a book or discussing a book with a title that makes them look bad or feel inferior. For example, below are some random titles to describe what I mean:

How to Control Your Undisciplined Kids

Get a Girlfriend in Seven Days or Less

The Low Self-Esteem Handbook

The Manly Art of Knitting

How to Raise Your I.Q.

Why God is Disappointed with You

The Life and Times of Hitler

The Best Dad is a Good Lover

The Beginner's Guide to Sex

The Zombie Raccoon Apocalypse

Yes, these titles might be funny on paper. But, most people wouldn't be caught dead reading a book in public with those titles. The discomfort of being seen reading a book with a weird title by other people is too palpable.

My point is to remind you that some titles can be deemed offensive, inappropriate, or in bad taste by readers. Sure, some book titles use provocative language with great success. But, there is a fine line you must walk. The reader's ego always has the final word. Why lose book sales by unknowingly making people feel uncomfortable?

Am I suggesting that you cower to the sophomoric tendencies of a reader's fragile ego? No, there is a much large factor to consider: word of mouth.

If people feel uncomfortable being seen with your book or discussing it with others, guess what happens? The word of mouth that you crave can come screeching to a halt. Most books are still sold via recommendations and word of mouth. Your title has the power to boost or diminish word of mouth. Thus, whenever you create a title for a book, ask some friends and readers in your target audience:

How would you feel if someone else saw you reading this book?

Always keep the reader ego in mind and make it work for you.

The One-Word Title Technique

When it comes to book titles, sometimes less is more. In fact, just one word can be a great option. Every week, there are numerous books with one-word titles on the *New York Times* bestseller list. Below are several examples:

Non-Fiction Bestsellers:

Boundaries

Collusion

Dopesick

Educated

Evicted

Fierce

Fighters

Nudge

Outliers

Principles

Quiet

Shaken

Unglued

Uninvited

Unhinged

Unbroken

When

Fiction Bestsellers:

Ambush

Artemis

Beartown

Bullseye

Burn

Cujo

Feared

Gone

Haunted

Insomnia

Instinct

It

Manhunt

Misery

Origin

Spymaster

Tailspin

Unraveled

Why consider using a single word to name your book? A one-word title is easiest for people to remember. It is also easier for readers to recite to friends. Plus, one word takes up the least amount of space on the cover art and marketing materials.

However, in order for a one-word title to be effective, the word you choose must generate a sense of emotion and curiosity. You could argue that any word is fair play. Yet, there are many words that naturally communicate a stronger sense of emotion than others. For instance, the words, "burn," "bulls-eye," and "cujo," convey more emotion than the words, "outlet," "grass," and "wallpaper."

If you decide to use a one-word title, keep in mind that your subtitle must be clear enough to explain your book's content and prevent confusion. For example, the non-fiction title, *Quiet*, could be confused with a novel, a music book, a book about deafness, etc. Therefore, the subtitle plays a key role to describe the exact content to readers. In the case of *Quiet*, the eloquent subtitle does a great job by stating, "The Power of Introverts in a World That Can't Stop Talking."

By the way, novels typically do not have subtitles, which is another reason why displaying a stellar hook on the back cover copy or online description is important. If you have a one-word title for a novel, the hook and synopsis must carry the marketing load.

When authors ask me how to create a one-word title, I typically walk them through this four-step technique:

Step 1 – Distill the main idea of your book into one or two sentences.

Step 2 – Create a list of individual words that relate to the main idea of your book. Could any of those words work as a provocative title? If not, go to Step 3.

Step 3 – Go to the website: http://www.Thesaurus.com and use this online tool to identify synonyms for the individual words you developed in Step 2. Create a list of potential candidates from the synonyms that you find. Examine if any of those synonym words could serve as an effective title.

Step 4 – If conducting Steps 1 – 3 does not produce a satisfactory option, try making up your own word that describes your book's content. Coining a new word can help get people's attention. For example, below is a list of bestselling titles using words that were made up:

Factfulness

Dopesick

Bossypants

Neverwhere

~

As I stated at the beginning of this chapter, there is no perfect title and there is no perfect method to create a title.

However, there is a commonsense principle you can always follow:

Never settle for a bland title.

Give your brain time to ruminate on various title options. Don't put unrealistic expectations on yourself to demand the right title during a 15-minute brainstorming session. Create different title options and let them percolate in your mind for a few weeks. Over time, the best ideas will usually rise to the surface, because they are provocative and catchy.

Moreover, allow yourself to let go of a working title that needs improvement. You may have to rewrite parts of your manuscript to fit a better title into your book, but the extra effort will pay dividends in the long run.

Just like fine wine takes time to mature, be patient and do the work to develop a title that attracts reader curiosity and is easy to remember.

Use the techniques listed in this chapter to develop various ideas. Tease the reader. Don't teach. Use my four questions to examine your options. Always be aware of reader ego. And, feel free to experiment with one-word titles.

For the legal eagles reading this book:

You may wonder if it's okay to copy the same title from another book. Legally, the answer is yes. In the United States, book titles are not protected under copyright law. To qualify for copyright protection, a book must possess "a significant amount of original expression." But, this term isn't fully defined by clear rules, and the court systems have ruled that "expressions" as short as book titles do not qualify for protection.

This doesn't mean that you are free to title your next book *The Chronicles of Narnia.* Some titles qualify for trademark protection, such as series titles like *The Lord of the Rings, Harry Potter, The Hunger Games,* etc. The U.S. Patent and Trademark Office states that a trademark protects "words, phrases, symbols or designs identifying the source of the goods or services of one party and distinguishing them from those of others." If a book becomes so successful that it is considered a recognizable brand, the title could be eligible for trademark protection.

For instance, if you title your book using the generic phrase, *The History of the World,* and another book shares that name, you are probably in the clear. But, if you decided to title a novel *The Da Vinci Code,* which is a specific title associated with a bestselling series, you should consider other title options in order to avoid potential lawsuits.

Fortunately, the English language is broad and diverse so that every author can develop multiple title ideas for a book that could be successful. Rather than be a copycat, let your creativity shine.

3

EXPLAIN YOUR BOOK PAYOFF WITH VALUE STATEMENTS

Note to novelists: The instruction in this chapter primarily applies to non-fiction books. However, I would advise that you still read the material, because it's always wise to gain a deeper perspective of how readers make book-buying decisions. Think of this chapter like getting extra credit in school. I'll even give you bonus points.

Since the dawn of the printing press, authors have carried a certain mystique within society. People tend to look at writers with fascination because they compose words that generate deep emotion or provide answers to frustrating problems. Authors are interviewed on national television. Authors are quoted as experts in newspapers and magazines. Authors are respected throughout worldwide culture.

Fair or not, this fascination leads many people to express admiration when meeting an author in person. This admiration is usually extended by asking typical questions, such as:

What is your book about?

Why did you write your book?

Tell me about the next book your writing.

These inquiries may sound simple, but they can generate a great deal of trepidation in the minds of most authors. For instance, when I pose those questions to unsuspecting authors, I typically receive a stuttering response, such as:

It's sort of about relationships and stuff like that.

I doubt you'll like my book. It's for a different audience.

The title is ___, and the book is about my title.

God told me to write a book.

Umm...I don't know.

The opportunity to tell someone about your book is the opportunity to sell a book. However, when someone asks what your book is about, you must be prepared to answer in a convincing manner. Remember, language is the power of the sale.

When authors cannot satisfy curious questions about the books they write, the problem is usually due to misunderstanding the actual question the other person is asking. This misinterpretation leads to a generic response that generates a disinterested look on the other person's face or a quick change of subject. Once you lose an opportunity to capture someone's interest in your book, it's tough to rekindle that interest.

To put it another way, here's what I encourage you to do whenever someone asks the question, "What is your book about?"

Never answer that question.

That's right. Never tell people what your book is about under any circumstances. Why? Because it's not the real question they want answered.

When someone asks you to tell them about your book, it's usually a smokescreen. They don't really want to know what your book is about. They are just being polite. In their minds, here is the real question people want you to answer:

What is in it for me?

To be more specific, people want to know if your book is worth the time and money to read. They are trying to determine if your book will entertain, inspire, or educate them in a satisfactory way. Since people have to buy a book before they can read it, they want an answer before they reach for their wallet or click the buy button online.

The harsh reality is that nobody cares what your book is about, the reasons why you wrote it, or why you might think it's great. If you could listen inside a person's mind, you would hear them think, "Is this book really in my self-interest? I don't want to waste my time and money. So, is your book really worth it?"

This dilemma doesn't just apply to people you meet in-person. Authors face the same challenge in every situation where people see their books. For example:

- When people look at your book on Amazon's website, they don't care what it is about. They want to know if it's worth purchasing.
- When people browse the shelves of a bookstore, they are wondering why they should choose your book over the hundreds of other titles in the room.
- When people see your books displayed on your author website, the split-second thought shoots through their mind, "What's in it for me?"
- When you promote your book on social media or in an email campaign, people aren't moved by your description. They are moved by their own self-interest.

This best way to solve these challenging questions is by providing persuasive answers that appeal to the reader's self-interest. I'll repeat it again: *language is the power of the book sale.*

For the rest of your author career, never tell people what your book is about. They don't care. Instead, learn how to answer the burning question within readers' minds. Tell people the payoff they will receive from reading your book.

Why People Decide to Buy a Book

People purchase books primarily based on their self-interest. This phenomenon drives the vast majority of purchases in the publishing industry. For example, when a reader feels satisfied after finishing an author's book, they tend to give that author the benefit of the doubt and buy their next book. This cycle explains why so many people continuously buy books from the same author, such as Michael Lewis, Jon Krakauer, Ann Coulter, David McCullough, etc. The same dynamic is true for mega-novelists, such as Agatha Christie, James Patterson, Danielle Steel, J.K. Rowling, etc. Books by these authors repeatedly satisfy the reader's self-interest.

Readers most commonly buy books from authors whom they already favor. This inclination occurs because the author's previous book delivered a satisfying outcome. Thus, the reader is willing to give the author another shot, because their self-interest was fulfilled in the past.

But, if you're a first-time author or an established author looking to expand your sales, you've got to sell more books to people who won't give you the benefit of the doubt. Their unfamiliarity with your writing means they're not sure your book will be a satisfying read. So, you face a stronger level of skepticism. The purpose of marketing is to help overcome that skepticism.

Thus, the key to effective book marketing language is to explain how your book will satisfy the reader. Your promotional text should be audience-focused, rather than self-focused. All of your book marketing materials, such as your website, back cover copy, personal bio, bookmarks, newsletters, and even social media posts, should explain how your books will entertain, inspire, or educate the reader.

People are asking you, "If I give you my money first, will your book give me something in return?" That return could be increased knowledge, a problem solved, or hours of entertainment reading a novel. But, it must be something that the reader deems worthy of their purchase.

If you display marketing text that tells readers the positive results they'll receive, you increase the chance of winning the book sale. I'm not saying that you'll win the sale every time. But, consider the alternative. If you fail to describe positive results or a satisfying outcome for the reader, you increase the odds of losing the book sale and winding up with the booby-prize of obscurity.

Don't make light of your marketing responsibility. It is the author's job to satisfy the reader's self-interest. Think of your audience's needs as much as your own. To identify the value of a non-fiction book, ask yourself these questions:

- How does your book inspire the reader?
- How does your book help the reader solve a problem?
- How does your book provide unique insights or a new perspective?
- How does your book offer entertainment or an escape from a busy day?

When I teach authors how to answer the questions above, I encourage them to write out their answers in the format of a value statement.

A "value statement" is an individual sentence that describes a specific result your book can create for readers. The perceived payoff is what makes your book valuable in a reader's eyes. A book's "value" is what readers pay to receive from the author.

In most cases, you should develop several value statements for your book. Your goal is to clearly explain how your message will benefit the reader. Here's an example of four value statements that I wrote for you as the reader of this book:

- I will help you sell more books.
- I will help you attract more readers without spending more money.
- I will help you create marketing language readers can't resist.
- I will help you enable fans to spread more word of mouth about your books.

Do those results sound good? They should, because I know it's what you want. How do I know? I'm an author myself, and I want the same results that you desire. How do I know that I can create these results for you? I've already trained hundreds of authors and successfully helped them experience these results. My value statements are based on fact, not hypothesis.

A value statement is not an attempt to guess at the results your book might provide. It's a declaration of your track record helping or entertaining other people. Every author should have a track record, even if you're a first-time author. How is that possible as a newbie?

Before you publish a book, put together a group of beta readers to test your manuscript and make sure that it delivers what they want. Your beta readers can serve as the start of your track record. However, there is an alarming trend among authors today to forego this step. It smacks of a lazy attitude or a careless indifference towards the reader. All around the world, every other major industry painstakingly tests their products before selling them to the public.

Before a chef offers a new menu at a fancy restaurant, he tests the recipes on the staff and beta customers. Before Hollywood studios release a new movie, they assemble focus groups and solicit feedback. Before technology companies launch new software, they recruit beta users to search for potential bugs. Before you bought this book, I asked several authors at different stages of their careers to review my manuscript material and help me improve it.

If focus groups and beta testers are used everywhere else, why avoid such an important step with your book? Beta testing means you no longer have to guess if your book will be considered worthwhile. You can know ahead of time that your book is good and why it is a satisfying read. Plus, the feedback you receive enhances your ability to create convincing value statements that sway more readers to purchase.

As you develop a track record of satisfying readers with your book, then you can write effective value statements based on the results that those readers receive. A value statement isn't a guess. It's a proclamation of the value that your book is meant to offer.

How to Write Value Statements in Four Steps

Here's a step-by-step process to create value statements for non-fiction books. Follow along with a pen and paper or set up a new file on your computer. Then, take a few minutes to walk through each part of this exercise:

Step 1 – List results that your book offers to readers

Write out separate sentences that explain individual results that your book delivers to your readers. Don't make guesses. You should be stating actual fact. Recall how readers described the benefits of reading your book. Restate positive comments from your beta readers. How do people describe feeling better off after having read your book?

Avoid trying to cram several results into one sentence. Break each result into a separate statement. You may end up with several value statements for each book (or even each chapter). That's fine. The more, the better. But, focus on the results that appeal to the largest segment of your book's intended audience.

Step 2 – Fill in the blank: "My book will help you: _____"

If you hit a wall attempting to describe your book's results, try this simple technique. First, write out this phrase:

My book will help you _____.

Then, fill in the blank with a specific result that your book will create for the reader. For example, you might fill in the blank with these types of results. My book will help you:

- Increase personal income so you can take more vacations.
- Raise kids who value education and develop a thirst to learn.
- Relive the battle of Normandy and feel like a soldier fighting in the trenches.

You can also try another approach to create value statements by filling in the blank to this sentence:

Imagine what your life would be like if _____.

- Imagine your life if you could wake up every day to your dream job.
- Imagine your life if you could enjoy marriage without arguing with your spouse.
- Imagine your life if you could become a master fly-fisherman. *(I'm still chasing that dream)*

Step 3 – Employ emotion

Logic makes people think, but emotion makes them act. So, you will connect with more readers if you explain your book's value on an emotional level. Avoid settling for value statements that are boring or use generic language. For instance, do you think the statements below sound appealing?

- My book will help people feel better.
- My book will help businesses run smoother.
- My book will help you live with confidence instead of fear.

Those statements may sound beneficial, but did they move you emotionally? No, those sentences are as bland as a vanilla wafer. To engage a reader's emotion, the value must specifically describe what the reader will feel. Below, I rewrote each bland statement from the list above to express more emotion:

- My book will help you regain the pain-free life that you used to enjoy.
- My book will help your company build teams that finish tasks fast with less conflict.
- My book will help you feel confident when stating your opinion and attract the respect of others.

See the difference? These statements are more effective due to the intensified emotion that is described. When you explain how readers will feel after reading your book, your marketing text will automatically become more appealing.

Step 4 – Use active words to emphasize results

Another way to enhance the impact of your value statements is by using active words that emphasize positive change. When you begin a value statement with an active word, it communicates how your book can increase something good or decrease something negative for the reader. Moving people from point A to point B, even just a little, can represent a helpful result.

For instance, reading a book by itself will not cause anyone to lose weight, mend a broken relationship, or get rid of their personal debt. But, the advice within a book can heighten a reader's awareness of medical, relational, and financial principles that enable the reader to overcome those challenges.

Consider how your book moves people in a positive direction. Below is a list of active words that serve as examples:

Increase, decrease, enhance, improve, strengthen, reduce, heighten, double, boost, raise, lower, etc.

Observe how the following value statements begin with active words that reflect a sense of positive change. My book will help you...

- *Strengthen* your ability to express genuine love to your spouse
- *Decrease* conflict by learning to build trust and resolve disagreements
- *Improve* productivity among employees with proper motivation
- *Enhance* your people skills to win more friends and energize your co-workers
- *Restore* adventurous dreams you have postponed

Active words help show how your book will increase something good or decrease something bad in the reader's life. The ability of your book to "increase" or "decrease" a tangible aspect of a person's life represents a result that people will pay to receive.

Now that we've covered the four steps to create value statements, begin developing several for each of your books. You will gain greater influence over readers when you clearly describe the results that your book will offer.

Value statements act as a convincing tool to address people who might be skeptical about your book. When people are riding the fence of indecision, they want proof that your book is worth purchasing. Your value statements give you the words to help get people off of the fence.

Other Sources of Inspiration for Value Statements

If you're a first-time author or new to concept of marketing, writing a value statement may feel uncomfortable at first. You may not be used to thinking about describing results for readers. If you hit a wall, flip the process and let readers tell you the positive results they've already experienced. Sometimes, the best value statements have already been said by your readers. You just need to find them. For example, try these four ideas for inspiration:

1. Review thank-you letters and emails from readers

Some people may send you a testimonial that describes a result your book created for them. If you see a pattern in the testimonials that you receive, that's a sign of consistent results. Use those comments to create value statements.

2. Examine the customer reviews for your book

Customer reviews on Amazon, Goodreads, and other websites can provide the seeds for excellent value statements. That's because the reviewer may specifically describe the benefits they received from your book. Copying the direct language from a satisfied reader can be used as convincing text to show other readers. Search through the reviews for your book to get ideas for value statements.

3. Reflect on the reasons you choose to write your book

Writing a book demands a lot of mental and emotional effort. Consider what moved you to undertake such a laborious task. Think about the central reasons why you were motivated to write your book. Had you recently overcome a challenge? Did you see injustice that needed to be addressed? Did you create new answers to a common problem? Were you moved by headlines that laid the foundation for a compelling story?

For instance, if you experienced a personal result in your own life that led you to write your book, then that same result is probably true for many of your readers. As the common adage says, "You've got to practice what you preach." Thus, examine how the message of your book improved your life. Then, use that knowledge to write powerful value statements for others.

4. Interview leaders within your target audience

If you write non-fiction, another way to uncover possible ideas for value statements is to interview leaders within your target audience. Ask them to describe the specific problems that their organizations face. Then, connect how the information in your book offers solutions to those issues. This is also a helpful way to conduct due diligence on your book and assure your material will provide value to the groups that need it the most.

5 Value Statement Pitfalls to Avoid

Before you display your value statements to the world, make sure they are effective. For example, you might think a value statement is persuasive, but readers may beg to differ. In this case, the reader's opinion is always right. If people aren't moved by your value statements, then you don't really have value statements. You just have an attempt that isn't working. If people do not respond with enthusiasm, then your value statements are not effective. Start over and try again.

Sometimes, your value statements can overlook mistakes that steal the thunder from your marketing text. Here are five pitfalls to avoid:

1. Avoid using clichés and ambiguous phrases

The most common problem I see with authors who struggle at writing value statements is using clichés or vague language. Examples might be sentences, such as "I will help you find peace in your heart" or "I will help you live in harmony with others."

These statements don't work, because they aren't specific enough to draw a person's interest. If your value statements sound cliché, readers won't be able to differentiate your book from the competition. The purpose of value statements is to make your book stand out from the pack and seem unique.

2. Avoid writing value statements that are teaching points

Condescending and preachy statements can be a turnoff to readers. For instance, the following statement sounds snooty, "My book will help you avoid feeling embarrassed when people see your kids in public." If your value statements make readers feel guilty or humiliated, you can erode their interest. Instead, describe a positive result that you know readers want, and make them feel like they will be the hero.

3. Avoid using technical terminology or religious expressions

For instance, religious authors can make the mistake of using unfamiliar language and weird words, such as "justification," "sanctification," "quiet-time," or "the world." Technology authors can fall into using lingo nobody understands, such as "data rates," "interface," or "scalability." These words are confusing to the uninitiated.

People won't buy your book if they don't understand the benefits you're trying to describe. Test your statements on someone who isn't a part of your religion or technology field. It's hard to evangelize people when they can't understand the words you're using.

4. Avoid too much negativity

Fear and dread are legitimate motivators in our society. But, most people are more intrigued by a positive result, rather than preventing something bad. For instance, this value statement concentrates too much on the negative, "My book will help you steer clear of destructive dating relationships." In contrast, people would be more willing to read a book with this value statement, "My book will help you find lasting love with the soul mate of your dreams."

5. Avoid long sentences that are hard to read

The principle of "less is more" also applies to value statements. If you take too long to describe your result, you can lose the reader's attention. I suggest keeping your value statements to less than 15 words in length. Sentences that are too long tend to become illegible and too hard to read. Plus, most marketing materials, such as back cover copy, author website page, or an Amazon book detail page, don't provide enough space to fit long sentences. Keep your value statements short and concise. Use brief, punchy phrases that grab the reader's attention.

Author Exercise: Write value statements for your books

Take each of your books and write 3 – 5 value statements for every title. Practice by beginning your sentences with "My book will help you _____."

Then, list your results as bulleted statements under each book title. If you come up with more than five, that's great. Just make sure that your statements represent real results that you've created for people – not hunches, guesses, or wishful thinking.

Where to Display Your Value Statements

By this point, you know the power that a value statement can bring to marketing your book. The next step is knowing where to use your value statements. I tell my clients, "Use them or lose them." Convincing language won't help you if people never see it. Below are five places where you want readers to see your value statements.

1. Weave value statements into your book description text

This topic is so important that I'm going to cover the details in the next chapter. For now, try to visualize the way that readers behave in a bookstore or browsing for new books online. Typically, they scan the front cover first and then read the book description text. In this moment, there is an opportunity to confirm a reader's interest and close the sale.

However, I'll be candid, most authors and publishers display bland text that works against the sale. The average description that I see for most books is a boring explanation of a non-fiction book's topic or a lifeless review of a novel's plot. No wonder so many books never break-even financially. If readers aren't engaged on an emotional level, they won't feel the need to purchase. Your book can win the battle by presenting descriptive text that captivates the reader's attention. We'll discuss this issue next in Chapter 4.

2. Add value statements to email and social media posts

When you create email campaigns or social media posts for your book, these activities represent an opportunity to remind recipients of the value they will receive. You must be concise, because most emails and social posts limit the amount of words you can show. But, that's why succinct value statements can be the perfect text to use.

Whenever you're in doubt about the right marketing text to display in an online promotion, especially for non-fiction books, fall back on this sure-fire, two-step method. First, use your marketing hook as described in Chapter 1. Second, follow your hook with a list of value statements. These two pieces of marketing language work hand-in-hand to get a reader's attention and confirm the payoff they'll receive from your book.

3. Add value statements to event promotional material

If you speak in public or conduct a lot of book signing events, value statements can help you draw a larger crowd. Before people take time out of their busy schedule to attend an event, they ask the same self-interested question, "What's in it for me?"

You can answer that question by adding value statements to your event promotional material. For instance, display a few value statements on your event registration form, email reminders, posters, brochures, etc. Spell out the results that attendees will receive by coming to your event.

4. Use value statements during personal conversations

Have you ever frozen mentally when someone asked you to tell them about your book? Our brains tend to lock up when we aren't sure how to answer a question. We stutter while trying to think of something clever to say. Or, we bumble our way through describing our book and cringe as we watch the other person feign interest. Believe me, I've made that mistake many times.

When you're talking to a potential reader in person, nobody wants to hear a boring description of your book. Remember, they are already skeptical. If the opportunity to discuss your book arises, here is the response I recommend: mention your marketing hook then follow it by reciting a few of your value statements.

Take time to memorize a few of your best value statements and keep them at the ready to recite whenever the need to explain your book arises. Concentrate on explaining how your content will either entertain or educate people. State your value statements with confidence knowing that you are answering the most important question being asked by the reader, "What's in it for me?"

If you commit your best value statements to memory, you'll never need to fear about freezing in the future. Nor will you have to worry about seeing a glazed look from people after they ask you about your book. Use persuasive language to turn the conversation in your favor.

Readers will always be too polite to directly ask you, "What's in it for me?" Nobody wants to sound overtly self-ish. Yet, every human buys books according to their self-interest. If your marketing text doesn't satisfy this perspective, then you will lose what every author wants the most – the reader's interest.

Use value statements to explain the specific results your book can help people experience. Recruit some beta readers to confirm your value if you're just getting started as a new author.

Logic makes people think, but emotion makes them act. Therefore, telling people about your book will make them think. But, emotionally describing the payoff of your book will make them buy.

Now that you've read this far, I hope that I've sufficiently answered the question you probably wondered before buying this book..."*What's in it for me?*"

4

WRITE A PERSUASIVE BOOK DESCRIPTION

We barely know each other, but may I ask you a personal question?

Why did you buy this book? Before you decided to purchase, did you read the marketing text on Amazon or review the back cover copy on the paperback?

Since you're reading this chapter, I assume the book description effectively captured your attention or connected on some level with a problem or felt need. For example, my book description begins with this hook:

Do you enjoy writing a book but hate writing the marketing text? Learn how to describe your book in ways that readers can't resist.

The rest of my book description touts my credentials as an expert and promises to help you learn important marketing skills, such as grabbing the reader's attention, creating clever titles, satisfying the reader's desire to buy. Obviously, my words succeeded in some capacity or you wouldn't be reading this book.

Likewise, I want to help you achieve the same goal of writing persuasive words that lead people to purchase. Your book description is a key component of this process. It may not be the only reason that people buy books. Of course, word of mouth, advertising, and author reputation play a large role in convincing readers to purchase. But, your book description is one area where you have the complete control to succeed. While you can't necessarily control other marketing factors, you can control the words you write.

The book description offers a golden opportunity to directly influence a reader's decision-making process. It's where your marketing hook, value statements, and plot description crystallize into one cohesive group. Plus, your book description appears in several pivotal places throughout the book-selling process, including:

- Back cover copy on a printed book
- Book detail page on Amazon and over 100 other online retailers
- Publisher and distributor catalog copy
- Publisher website
- Author website

Based on all of the places people may see your book description, you need to think seriously about the marketing text that you create. You usually get 150 – 300 words capture the reader's interest, so your words must count. When written well, great marketing copy can close a lot of extra book sales by itself.

In my opinion, the author is responsible for writing the book description, not the publisher. Why rely on someone else to do the job? That's like letting someone else name your baby. Your book is your baby, so you should write the description.

You could argue that I'm over-reacting, but I'd argue that a casual view of writing your book description means wasting easy opportunities to sell more books. As my poker-playing uncle used to say, "Never leave money on the table!"

Have you left money on the table due to bland marketing text with your previous books? You know the description could be better. That's okay. Maybe you didn't know how to fix it until now. Or, maybe you sold enough books in the past to feel satisfied. Either way, it's never too late to improve your craft as a writer.

Rather than leave more money on the table, let's learn how to turn the tables and secure extra sales for free. Improving your book description doesn't cost a dime. It just takes a little work and the desire to master the art of language. In that regard, this chapter will explain how to:

- Understand what makes a stellar book description
- Follow step-by-step templates to create a nonfiction or fiction book description
- Think like a reader who is unfamiliar with your book

Special Bonus:

If you're a traditionally-publisher author, you might be concerned that the marketing text for your books cannot be changed on Amazon, the largest online book retailer. Maybe your publisher wrote a bland description for your book and uploaded it to Amazon for the world to see. Are you stuck with everyone looking at subpar text forever? Can someone save your book from this marketing misery?

There is hope! As of this writing, there is a way to override your publisher and update your book description on Amazon by yourself. This little-known technique enables any author to access Amazon's website, find their books, and upload new marketing text. Hang tight. In Chapter 7, I'll walk you through the steps to access Amazon's secret "back door" for authors. Best of all, it's free.

Aren't you glad you bought this book?

Stellar Example of a Nonfiction Book Description

Just like creating a title, there is no perfect method to develop a persuasive book description. But, if this is your first time, or if you've struggled to write convincing copy in the past, I recommend looking at stellar examples to know where the industry bar is set. It can be difficult to create an excellent book description when you've never seen one.

Let's review examples of outstanding nonfiction and fiction book descriptions. Don't let these exceptional examples intimidate you. I will break down how to apply what works to your book. First, we'll look at the nonfiction book description for *Getting Past No* by William Ury. Then, we'll look at the synopsis for the novel, *The Girl on the Train*, by Paula Hawkins.

One of my favorite descriptions of a nonfiction book is for *Getting Past No: Negotiating In Difficult Situations*. Use the link below if you'd like to view the marketing text on Amazon's website:

https://www.amazon.com/dp/0553371312

Below is a copy of the book description. Read it for yourself and see if you agree that the words are effective:

We all want to get to yes, but what happens when the other person keeps saying no?

How can you negotiate successfully with a stubborn boss, an irate customer, or a deceitful coworker?

In Getting Past No, William Ury of Harvard Law School's Program on Negotiation offers a proven breakthrough strategy for turning adversaries into negotiating partners. You'll learn how to:

- *Stay in control under pressure*
- *Defuse anger and hostility*
- *Find out what the other side really wants*
- *Counter dirty tricks*
- *Use power to bring the other side back to the table*
- *Reach agreements that satisfies both sides' needs*

Getting Past No is the state-of-the-art book on negotiation for the twenty-first century. It will help you deal with tough times, tough people, and tough negotiations. You don't have to get mad or get even. Instead, you can get what you want!

Wow! That's what I call a persuasive book description. Kudos to the author, William Ury, and his publisher, Bantam Books. The description for *Getting Past No* displays a compelling hook and clearly communicates the payoff for the reader. I'll explain why the text works so well later in this chapter when we discuss my nonfiction book description template. However, let's switch gears and look at a stellar description for a novel.

Stellar Example of a Fiction Book Description

For novels, I'm a big fan of the book description for *The Girl on the Train* by Paula Hawkins. To see the text in action, use the link below to view the book on Amazon's website:

https://www.amazon.com/dp/1594634025

Like the nonfiction book we just reviewed, the synopsis for this novel displays persuasive marketing text that is irresistible:

The Girl on the Train is the debut psychological thriller from Paula Hawkins that will forever change the way you look at other people's lives, from the author of Into the Water.

EVERY DAY THE SAME

Rachel takes the same commuter train every morning and night. Every day she rattles down the track, flashes past a stretch of cozy suburban homes, and stops at the signal that allows her to daily watch the same couple breakfasting on their deck. She's even started to feel like she knows them. Jess and Jason, she calls them. Their life—as she sees it—is perfect. Not unlike the life she recently lost.

UNTIL TODAY

And, then she sees something shocking. It's only a minute until the train moves on, but it's enough. Now everything's changed. Unable to keep it to herself, Rachel goes to the police. But is she really as unreliable as they say? Soon she is deeply entangled not only in the investigation but in the lives of everyone involved. Has she done more harm than good?

Bravo to Paula and her publisher, Riverhead Books! The book description for *The Girl on the Train* is compelling. The marketing hook grabs your attention and the synopsis ends with a suspenseful cliffhanger. You can feel the emotion that the reader will experience within the author's story.

If you enjoy reading suspense, the payoff from the book is apparent. I also like the clever mention and cross-promotion of the author's next book, *Into the Water*. This marketing language is like a freight train that drives the book sale.

Now that we've analyzed examples of top-notch book descriptions, let's boil down the process using step-by-step templates to aid the process. The following sections provide separate templates for nonfiction and novels. Let's start with nonfiction first.

Note about memoirs: If you're writing a nonfiction memoir,

I suggest using my fiction template to create your book description. In most cases, the dramatic story of someone's life within a memoir has more in common with marketing a novel than a nonfiction book.

Write a Nonfiction Book Description in 5 Easy Steps

In order for a nonfiction book description to be successful, the marketing language must resonate with the reader in two ways:

- Understand how the reader feels
- Understand what the reader wants

When people consider buying a nonfiction book, they are usually motivated by an internal desire to solve a problem, learn something new, or feel more inspired. However, logic makes people think, but emotion makes them act. If you can identify the feeling that is motivating the reader, then you create an emotional connection that makes the reader think, "This author understands me."

When readers believe that you understand how they feel, they become more open to the solution offered within your book. This opens the door to explain how you understand what they want, which is the desired payoff that we discussed in the previous chapter regarding value statements.

In its simplest form, your book description is meant to show readers that you understand how they feel and recognize what they want. To address these two goals, use the following five-step template to walk through the process. I'll describe each step of the template. Then, I'll apply the template to *Getting Past No*, so that you can see the five steps in action.

Step 1 – Start with a marketing hook

Always start your book description with a marketing hook. Make it stand out as a separate sentence from the rest of your text. You must get people's attention before you can tell them anything else about your book. If you fail to get the reader's attention, the next four parts of your book description will be wasted (If necessary, return to Chapter 1 for details on creating a hook.)

Step 2 – Tell the reader you know how they feel

In the second step, tell the reader that you understand how they feel. In most cases, you wrote your non-fiction book to address a problem or a felt need that people want to resolve. State how you understand that problem or felt need in 1 – 2 sentences. This step allows people to recognize why your book is worth considering. To show people you know what they are feeling, use these fill-in-the-blank phrases as idea starters, such as:

Are you tired of _____?

Do you wish you could _____?

Do you love ____, but hate ____?

The number one problem today is _____.

You want _____, but instead _____ happens.

Step 3 – Tell the reader you know what they want

Once readers agree that you know how they feel, they become emotionally open to the payoff your book can provide. Thus, the third step is to explain the value and results offered by your book. You are essentially explaining that you know what they want.

Complete this part of the template by inserting the value statements for your book. For a refresher on creating value statements, see Chapter 3. Or, use these questions and phrases below to spark ideas for creating new value statements:

My book will help you _____.

How will your book specifically improve the reader's condition?

How will your book educate or inspire the reader?

What specific results will readers experience from applying your book to their lives?

I recommend displaying 3 – 6 value statements as a bulleted list within your book description. You want the payoff from your book to be easily seen by readers. If they miss seeing the payoff, you might miss the book sale. You'll see examples of good value statements in the next section when we apply this template to the book, *Getting Past No.*

Step 4 – Tell the reader you can be trusted

The fourth step is meant to address skepticism that can linger in people's minds if they have never heard of you or your book. Many readers can wonder, "Can I trust this author with my time and money?" If they remain uncertain, their skepticism can cost you the book sale. So, the next step in this template is to minimize doubt by describing your credibility and showing readers that they can trust you. For example, you could mention the following credentials:

- Professional certifications, such as Ph.D., CPA, AIA, M.D., LMFT, etc.
- Professional or industry awards, such as Who's Who, Top 30 under 30, etc.
- Job title, such as President, Founder, Professor, Vice President, Director, etc.
- Past experience, such as 10 or 25 years working in a particular field
- Bestselling author of _____
- Author whose books have sold over 50,000, 100,000, or 1 million copies.
- Local or regional awards, such as Winner of the Texas Writer's Book Award

People won't know about your experience and credentials unless you display them. You don't have to be a Ph.D. to convince readers, just give enough information to build trust.

Step 5 – End with a Call to Action

A persuasive book description should finish with a bang, rather than a whimper. Tell the reader to buy your book. You may think this step is a crass or unnecessary, but nothing could be further from the truth. Never forget how easy it is for a shopper on Amazon to leave your book page and buy a different book instead.

When you have the reader's attention, don't trip at the finish line. Use this last step to close the sale by telling the reader to purchase. It doesn't mean you're insulting their intelligence. Instead, you are reinforcing the idea that buying your book is a good choice that shouldn't be delayed. Feel free to use language that fits your personality. But, display some type of call to action for people to see. Otherwise, you will miss out on extra sales that you could easily close. For example, use phrases like these below to prompt the reader:

Buy your copy today.

Enjoy reading "insert your title."

Get it now.

Experience these results today.

Buy a copy of "insert your title."

When put the five steps of the template together, you have a complete process to write an effective nonfiction book description:

Step 1 – Start with a marketing hook

Step 2 – Tell the reader you know how they feel

Step 3 – Tell the reader you know what they want

Step 4 – Tell the reader you can be trusted

Step 5 – Give a call to action

To see these steps in action, observe how they appear in the book description for *Getting Past No*. For example, the description starts with an effective Step 1 marketing hook:

We all want to get to yes, but what happens when the other person keeps saying no?

This question works as a marketing hook, because readers who want to improve their negotiation skills will see those words and think, "Yes, I keep getting confounded when people tell me no. Okay, you've got my attention."

Next, the book description moves to Step 2 by specifically describing issues the reader is feeling:

How can you negotiate with a stubborn boss, an irate customer, or a deceitful co-worker?

Almost everyone can relate to those problems described above. So, the reader thinks, "This author understands what I feel."

The next part of this book description reverses Steps 3 and 4 of my template, but the text still works effectively. Since William Ury has an impressive bio teaching at Harvard University, his credibility based on Step 4 is moved earlier in the book description and validated by the next sentence:

William Ury of Harvard Law School's Program on Negotiation offers a proven breakthrough strategy for turning adversaries into negotiating partners.

Lastly, the book description concludes by explaining how the author understands what the reader wants. This step presents an excellent list of bullet points and a closing paragraph that specifically describes the payoff for the reader. Plus, the last sentence covers Step 5, which displays a persuasive call to action:

You will learn how to:

- *Stay in control under pressure*
- *Defuse anger and hostility*
- *Find out what the other side really wants*
- *Counter dirty tricks*
- *Use power to bring the other side back to the table*
- *Reach agreements that satisfies both sides' needs*

Getting Past No is the state-of-the-art book on negotiation for the twenty-first century. It will help you deal with tough times, tough people, and tough negotiations. You don't have to get mad or get even. Instead, you can get what you want!

If someone reading this text desires to improve their negotiation skills, you can see how this book description presents a potent reason to buy a copy.

If you write nonfiction, especially educational or self-help content, use this five-step template as a guide to follow. Start with an attention-grabbing hook, describe the felt need, explain the exciting payoff, define your author credibility, and close with a call to action.

Write a Fiction Book Description in 3 Easy Steps

If you write novels, you can create a persuasive book

description or "synopsis" using this three-step template. I'll weave the marketing text from our earlier example, *The Girl on the Train*, to show how the steps work together.

- Step 1 – Display your book hook
- Step 2 – Describe your main character in conflict
- Step 3 – Close with a cliffhanger

Step 1 – Display your book hook

Every book description, including fiction, should start with a captivating hook. Otherwise, how will you grab people's attention? If you need a quick refresher, refer back to Chapter 1 for instructions on creating hooks. Think like a screenwriter pitching a movie in one sentence or try the "What if I told you" technique. For our example, the marketing hook for *The Girl on the Train* is:

EVERY DAY THE SAME...UNTIL TODAY.

I appreciate the simplicity of this short hook and the power of presenting the words in all caps, which is optional.

As a side note, if you review the book description for *The Girl on the Train* on Amazon's website, you may notice the hook sentence is split over two paragraphs to add a visual effect. This approach is also optional. As long as readers can clearly see the arresting hook, then you can grab people's attention.

Step 2 – Describe your main character in conflict

After displaying your hook in Step 1, the next step is to describe your main character experiencing intense conflict.

Almost every genre of fiction involves a story where the protagonist is thrown into an extreme level of strife, confusion, or danger. The settings may be different, the hero and villain personalities may be diverse, but every great story revolves around the main character trying to resolve conflict and achieve a goal. It is the conflict that attracts the reader's interest.

Therefore, it is your goal in Step 2 to describe emotional conflict to the point where the reader can feel it, too. In other words, it is not your goal to explain the whole story or give a boring overview of your setting and all the characters involved. Keep this point in mind:

Don't tell people about your story. Tell people about the conflict.

If your synopsis doesn't make readers feel the conflict, then your description is too bland. Logic makes people think, but emotion makes them act. If you want more readers to buy your novel, make them feel the emotional angst. In fact, show your synopsis to a few people and ask them if they feel anything when they read it. If not, you've got a dead synopsis. Start over and crank up the conflict even more.

You can develop emotional conflict for your synopsis from multiple places in your story. In many cases, you can describe the turmoil that the main character experiences in the opening scene. For example, the synopsis of *The Girl on the Train* opens with some basic information about the setting and the protagonist, Rachel. But, the description quickly moves to the turmoil that unfolds after she sees something shocking in the beginning of the story:

Rachel takes the same commuter train every morning and night. Every day she rattles down the track, flashes past a stretch of cozy suburban homes, and stops at the signal that allows her to daily watch the same couple breakfasting on their deck. She's even started to feel like she knows them. Jess and Jason, she calls them. Their life—as she sees it—is perfect. Not unlike the life she recently lost.

And, then she sees something shocking. It's only a minute until the train moves on, but it's enough. Now everything's changed. Unable to keep it to herself, Rachel goes to the police.

Most novelists are smart to plunge the protagonist into major conflict right away, because that's what draws the reader into the story. Thus, describe this conflict from your opening section for Step 2 of your synopsis.

However, there may be cases where the most intense conflict occurs in the middle or end of the story. That may also be a good option. But, if you choose to pull conflict from those latter sections, be careful in your description to avoid giving away clues that could spoil the conclusion.

Whether you write romantic beach reads, cozy mysteries, action thrillers, or gory horror stories, your goal is to weave dramatic conflict into your book description. Once the reader can feel the turmoil of the protagonist, then you're ready to close the sale with Step 3.

Step 3 – Close with a cliffhanger

Every reader knows that a novel is completely scripted by the author. But, if you tease readers properly, they will gladly pay money to find out what happens. That's the purpose of Step 3. Tease readers to the point where they must find out the ending.

You achieve this goal by writing a cliffhanger question or sentence that leaves the reader hanging on the edge of their seat.

Will the protagonist find true love?

Will the villain be stopped?

Will justice be served?

He broke her dreams. Now she's going to break his heart.

Now he's mad and it's payback time.

Always close your synopsis with a cliffhanger. This step is vitally important. Lead the reader wonder what will happen next. For example, the description of *The Girl on the Train* ends with a provocative question:

But is Rachel really as unreliable as they say? Soon she is deeply entangled not only in the investigation but in the lives of everyone involved. Has she done more harm than good?

That's what I call a cliffhanger ending. If you enjoy reading suspense, you're hooked. You've got to find out what happens.

A good cliffhanger can also serve as the "call to action," similar to Step 5 that I mentioned earlier in my nonfiction template. But, it can be wise to include a straightforward call to action at the end of your description that capitalizes on the reader's interest, such as:

Buy a copy today and find out what happens.

Get your copy today.

Purchase "insert your title" and find out what happens next.

Buy "insert your title" now.

Whether you're a budding novelist or a veteran bestseller, this three-step template can work for your synopsis. Grab the reader's attention with a hook, describe the main character in conflict, then close with a cliffhanger.

Are there other ways to create a great book description? Of course. I'm not here to tell you that there is only one way. You may develop a completely different approach that motivates readers to purchase. If it works, go with it.

But, if you've never written a book description, or if you feel stuck in a rut writing descriptive copy, use these templates as a guide to rekindle your creative juices.

Think Like a Newbie and Recruit Beta Readers

I may be an expert marketing consultant, but I'll admit that I'm not perfect. Sometimes, all of my experience works against me. Even though I've coached hundreds of writers and worked with numerous bestsellers, my knowledge can cause me to forget something very important – the perspective of a first-time author.

Here's an example. After I developed the initial marketing copy for my book, *The Author's Guide to Email Marketing*, I sent it to my group of beta readers expecting to receive a positive response. After all, I'm the marketing expert, right? Instead, the opposite happened. I got a lot of negative feedback.

Several of my beta readers responded that my book description didn't resonate with them. They said I used technical terms that they didn't understand, such as "automated onboarding sequence" and "GDPR regulations." They also stated that my synopsis sounded like the book was written only for experienced authors, rather than first-time authors.

I was shocked – not by their comments, but by my egregious mistake. I had forgotten to put myself in the shoes of a new author who is unfamiliar with the jargon of the publishing industry. Due to my years of experience, my brain was automatically using publishing lingo. I didn't write my marketing text while keeping the perspective of a new author in mind. Therefore, my initial book description was difficult to understand and felt out of touch with the average reader's needs. Fortunately, with their help, I revised the marketing copy to a much better level.

Don't make my mistake. Instead, when your write your book description, abide by this simple principle:

Always keep the newbie in mind.

In any given book genre, "newbies" typically outnumber the aficionados and the heavy readers. A "newbie" is someone who is trying something new to see if they like it. They are the opposite of readers who are immersed in a genre or devoted as a fan to a specific author. Thus, if you want to sell more books, don't overlook the largest segment of potential readers – the newbies.

However, newbies are not only new, they also represent a different kind of reader. Their "newness" means they are unfamiliar with an established group's lingo, behavior, or customs. They won't appreciate jargon that adoring fans are able to understand.

For example, if you write nonfiction, your book description should avoid technical terms that would go right over a newbie's head. Otherwise, you can lose book sales due to sounding overly complex or out of touch with the uninitiated.

If you write fiction, many people who read your synopsis won't be familiar with your main character, setting, or writing style. They are "newbies" to the worlds within your stories. As you create your book description, put yourself in the shoes of someone who is a novice to your novels. There are always more newbies than avid readers.

Here's an exercise to test if your book description works well for newbies: Enlist a group of beta readers and include a few people are unfamiliar with your genre. They might be friends, co-workers, neighbors, or authors who write in a different genre than you. Seek out a few newbies who agree to read your marketing text and provide honest feedback. Their response could be invaluable to improving your marketing copy.

A good group of beta readers can help you develop marketing language that appeals to a wider range of readers. Sometimes, it's difficult for experienced authors to create this type of language, because we get too deep into our own material. As the old adage says, "We can't see the forest for the trees."

Use beta readers who are outside of "your forest" and will alert you to issues that make your book description unappealing. Their feedback can help secure more book sales, because they provide the perspective that other newbies would understand. In essence, your beta readers can teach you how to sell to the uninitiated.

If you've felt uneasy that your book description was weak, overcome the problem by seeking feedback from beta readers who can give a broader context. The largest number of book buyers for most genres are newbies. Think like a newcomer and talk with newbies. Then, you'll market your book with a higher level of confidence.

Once you've written a persuasive book description, a wonderful time-saving benefit occurs. You won't have to reinvent the wheel every time you need effective marketing text to promote your book. You've already got it. Pull from the elements of your book description. It's like a one-stop-stop for finding convincing promotional copy. For instance, your book description can be repackaged and reused in various situations, such as:

- Use your book hook and value statements on Facebook, BookBub, or Amazon ads

- Insert your book description into email campaigns
- Send your publisher top-notch back cover copy to use with retailers
- Begin a media interview with your book hook and value statements
- Add your book description to the byline at the end of blog posts and articles
- Promote your book on your author website

Wring the maximum value out of writing a great book description. Use it again and again. People never get tired of hearing convincing language. Never get tired of using it.

5

DISPLAY DRAMATIC ACCOLADES ON AMAZON

I have a confession to make. In the previous chapter, I lied to you. Well, maybe not an actual lie. But, I withheld some important information. You might say that I "told a story."

In Chapter 4, we used the novel, *The Girl on the Train*, as a stellar example of how to create a fiction book description. Then, I explained how the text coincided with my three-step template to help novelists write an effective synopsis. However, I was not entirely forthcoming. While the synopsis is excellent, I didn't show you the best marketing text for *The Girl on the Train*. I showed you the actual book description, but there is more to the marketing story.

Now, it's time to come clean. I want to show you the rest of the marketing text for *The Girl on the Train*. Below is the complete Amazon description that people see when viewing the book on Amazon's website. The text is in bold, just like the way it appears on Amazon:

. . .

The #1 *New York Times* bestseller, *USA Today* Book of the Year, now a major motion picture starring Emily Blunt.

The debut psychological thriller that will forever change the way you look at other people's lives, from the author of *Into the Water.*

"Nothing is more addicting than *The Girl on the Train.*"—*Vanity Fair*

"*The Girl on the Train* has more fun with unreliable narration than any chiller since *Gone Girl*...[It] is liable to draw a large, bedazzled readership."—*The New York Times*

"Marries movie noir with novelistic trickery...hang on tight. You'll be surprised by what horrors lurk around the bend."—*USA Today*

"Like its train, the story blasts through the stagnation of these lives in suburban London and the reader cannot help but turn pages."—*The Boston Globe*

"*Gone Girl* fans will devour this psychological thriller."—*People Magazine*

To see all of this marketing copy on Amazon, use this link:

https://www.amazon.com/dp/1594634025

Okay, I apologize for my little ruse. But, I ask you...now that you've seen all of these accolades, how do you feel about *The Girl on the Train*? Do you view the novel in a different light than you did in Chapter 4? Do you believe these bestseller awards and major endorsements would convince more people to buy the book? Maybe you're jaded and think the achievements don't matter. Here's the real question:

Would you want your book to appear on Amazon with all of those accolades?

Of course, you would. Every author wants to see their book receive praise. An author would have to be crazy to eschew that level of notoriety.

However, if I had shown you the accolades for the *Girl on the Train* in Chapter 4, your perspective of the synopsis would have been different, right? Those achievements would have affected your opinion of the book. That's why I kept them separate without telling you first. I wanted you to *feel* the difference between seeing a book with accolades versus a book description without accolades.

Accolades are another form of marketing text that helps sell books. In some cases, powerful accolades can be more persuasive than any clever hook, title, or book description you might create. The problem is that accolades are usually beyond your control. You have to wait for them to be bestowed upon your book. But, if you earn an award or receive a major testimonial, you have the control to let the world know. Thus, the purpose of this chapter is to cover these topics:

- Why accolades help sell more books
- Why accolades matter on Amazon
- Where to display your accolades on Amazon
- What to do if you don't have any accolades

In Chapter 7, I'll reveal how to access Amazon's website and update your book with new accolades and better marketing text whenever you desire.

As an aside: If you happen to work for a publishing house and you're reading this book, I highly recommend you use the advice in this chapter. Updating the books you publish with industry accolades on Amazon can result in extra revenue for your company – for free.

Why Accolades Matter on Amazon

At the time of this writing, Amazon literally dominates the publishing industry. Take a moment to consider these mind-blowing statistics:

- Amazon sells close to 50% of all print books in America.
- Amazon sells over 70% of all e-books in America.
- Amazon is the largest sales account for almost every publisher in America.
- Amazon paid 1,000 indie authors over $100,000 each in book royalties in 2017.
- Amazon's market share continues to increase as their competition struggles.

Sources:

http://authorearnings.com/report/february-2017/

http://authorearnings.com/report/dbw2017/

https://bit.ly/2qGKiOl

If these Amazon facts don't get your attention, allow me to make things very clear:

Amazon sells more books than anyone else. If you want to sell more books, then learn how to sell more books on Amazon.

It doesn't matter if you're self-published or traditionally-published. It doesn't matter if you write fiction or non-fiction. It doesn't matter if you're a first-time author or an experienced bestseller. Today, success for every author hinges upon selling more books on Amazon. To help you take full advantage of Amazon's power, I encourage to read my book, *The Author's Guide to Marketing Books on Amazon.* You will find that resource helpful.

However, this guide is all about how to write text that sells books. Let's put two and two together. If readers buy books on Amazon more than anywhere else, then maximizing the way your books appear on Amazon is critical. If you display persuasive text on their website, you can lead more people to make a purchase. Whereas, if your book has lackluster marketing text on Amazon, it will negatively affect your sales.

So far, I've explained how to develop an effective hook, attractive title, value statements, and a persuasive book description. But, as I just revealed in the example of *The Girl on the Train*, there is another form of promotional text that can sway Amazon shoppers to purchase: *accolades*.

Fortunately, Amazon makes it possible to tout special awards, milestones, and endorsements to help your book stand out from the crowd. You may not be able to update your book cover. But, you can always change your book description. Chapter 7 will explain how to upload your most up-to-date achievements to Amazon.

Yet, too many authors who receive accolades never add those accomplishments to their books on Amazon. Thus, shoppers just view those books like any other run-of-the-mill title.

Many publishers make the same mistake, so you can't rely on them to keep your books updated on Amazon. For example, I conducted a research study for a mid-sized publishing house and found that over 50 of their *New York Times* bestselling books never had that accolade added to the detail page on Amazon - for years. Over 50! That means thousands, possibly millions, of Amazon shoppers never knew they were looking at 50 *New York Times* bestsellers while browsing on Amazon. Imagine how many extra sales could have been captured if the publisher had kept the accolades for those books up to date. Imagine how you would feel as the author to discover this marketing faux pas.

This type of marketing mistake is like owning a sports car but never driving it fast. Or, a woman who gets engaged but never wears her ring. Or, a team that wins a championship but never displays the trophy. You get my point.

If you've got accolades, flaunt them – especially on Amazon. Not in a prideful way, but in a fact-based, convincing way. For example, I've already made sure that you know I've helped books hit the *New York Times* bestseller list in three different categories. I don't tell you that accomplishment to brag. I tell you in order to prove that you're listening to an experienced professional who is credible.

Readers shopping on Amazon respond to accolades because they prefer to buy and read books that have a satisfying reputation. This explains why you see books touting "*New York Times* bestseller" or authors proclaiming to be a *USA Today* or *Wall Street Journal* bestseller. Accolades help confirm that your book should be perceived as a high-quality item that shoppers should value.

Consider another important fact about Amazon. There are over 30,000,000 paperback books available to purchase on their website. That number doesn't include all of the e-books, hardcovers, and audio books for sale. How can your book compete on Amazon against millions of other titles?

Use accolades to make your book stand out from the crowd.

If your book has achieved an extra level of credibility, you would be remiss to withhold that persuasive information from shoppers. Instead, do everything possible to differentiate your book from the competition. Displaying legitimate accolades on Amazon will help you close more book sales.

Amazon Makes You Work for People's Attention

Do you have a book for sale on Amazon's website? If so, take a moment to review your book detail webpage. Look at the section where your book description is displayed. You may notice that Amazon doesn't make it easy for people to read all of your marketing text. Their website only shows the first 30 – 40 words of your description.

This short word count depends on the size of your computer screen and the device you're using. But, it rarely equates to more than three sentences or four lines of text. That's not much space nor many words to get people's attention. After those 30 – 40 initial words, Amazon covers up the rest of your book description and displays a small link that says, "Read more." This link presents a challenge.

If your first 30 – 40 words don't interest the reader, then they usually won't click on the "Read more" link and review the rest of your book description. If they choose not to read more about your book, they probably aren't interested in buying a copy.

Put simply, Amazon forces you to earn people's attention. That's the challenge. The first few words that shoppers see about your book need to be enticing. Also, those words need to stand out on a busy Amazon page already cluttered with other information vying for a shopper's attention. When you've only got a tiny space and a few words to get people's attention, what is your best bet for success?

Display convincing accolades.

Five Effective Accolades to Use on Amazon

In the latter part of Chapter 1, I talked about the importance of creating a book hook and displaying that hook at the top of your book's Amazon page. The purpose of the hook is to grab people's attention and lead them into the rest of your book description.

But, there is another way to hook people's attention besides using the "What if I told you" or "movie screenwriter" techniques that I described in Chapter 1. A great hook can also be achieved by displaying any of the following accolades:

1. National bestseller status

If your book has hit a high-profile national bestseller list, shout that achievement from the rooftops. Display those words at the very top of your book page on Amazon.

Legitimate national bestseller lists include the *New York Times, USA Today, Publishers Weekly,* and *The Wall Street Journal.* Making it onto to those lists immediately boosts your book's status and credibility among average readers. Bestseller lists act like a digital form of word of mouth. For example, when some readers see that a book is a *New York Times* bestseller, they interpret that accomplishment as a believable recommendation from the *New York Times.* If that reader trusts the *New York Times* and agrees their bestseller lists validate books worth reading, then they will purchase based upon seeing the book make the list.

In fact, Peter Hildick-Smith of the Codex Group, who specializes in publishing industry research, told me that his studies have shown around 5% of book consumers in America buy books based on the bestseller lists. Also, it is a known fact that libraries order books that hit the *New York Times* bestseller list, because requests for those books from patrons immediately increases. The national bestseller lists act as a direct recommendation that many readers trust.

Heck, my wife's book club usually selects their books to discuss based on the bestseller lists. It's so much easier to say, "We should all read this book. It's a *New York Times* bestseller." Uttering that phrase causes numerous copies of the same book to be purchased by a group.

Are the bestseller lists rigged? Absolutely. It's even possible for authors to buy their way onto the bestseller lists – for around $200,000. But, that's a different discussion for another time. The bottom line is that bestseller lists move some people to purchase books. Not everyone, of course. But, enough people that you'd be crazy to achieve that status and keep it to yourself.

If your book is a bona-fide bestseller, put that accolade at the top of your Amazon page using BIG BOLD LETTERS.

2. Endorsements from well-known people

Your book may not have hit a bestseller list, but you might have a major endorsement from a well-known leader, athlete, musician, politician, or celebrity. If so, put that testimonial at the top of your book detail page as an effective marketing hook for people to see.

For example, the book, *Factfulness*, by Hans Rosling has an endorsement from Bill Gates displayed on the book's Amazon page. Below is the actual recommendation:

"Factfulness is one of the most important books I've ever

read—an indispensable guide to thinking clearly about the world." – **Bill Gates**

As the founder of Microsoft and one of the richest men in the world, Bill Gates is so famous and well-respected that many people will buy *Factfulness* based on his recommendation alone. His endorsement serves as a compelling marketing hook. It's the ultimate version of word of mouth. It makes sense to display his testimonial at the top for the world to see. View his words in action on Amazon using this link:

https://www.amazon.com/dp/1250107814

Just in case you're reading this section and feel frustrated that you don't have major testimonials or bestseller status, stay with me. I'll address those concerns at the end of this chapter.

3. Major sales milestones

Another example of an effective accolade that impresses readers is surpassing a sales milestone. For example, if your book has sold over 100,000 copies, or especially 1 million copies, those numbers represent impressive achievements that cause readers to take notice.

The milestone acts like a hook to get people's attention and imply, "Look at how many other people have bought this book. You can trust the collective action of over 100,000 people. Therefore, you will like this book, too."

Surprisingly, many authors lose track of their sales and fail to keep these influential numbers updated for shoppers to see. Displaying a sales milestone persuades people to purchase. In addition, it's a great technique to keep interest in a backlist book that has been in circulation for several years. Show people that an older book is still relevant by displaying the significant sales that have been achieved.

4. Reviews from high-profile media outlets

When I displayed the accolades for *Girl on the Train* at the beginning of this chapter, there was also a list of blurbs from major media outlets who review books, including the *New York Times, Vanity Fair, People, The Boston Globe*, etc. There are dozens of other national newspapers, regional newspapers, online media sites, and magazines that review books on a respected level.

There are so many books in the marketplace that shoppers cannot wade through every title to make a buying decision. Therefore, many readers lean on trusted reviewers and major book club recommendations to decide what to buy. If your book receives praise from a professional reviewer, let the world see it.

5. Literature awards

To a lesser degree, winning or being nominated for a literary award also serves as an accolade that hooks some readers' attention. The average reader is unfamiliar with most literary awards. But, if your genre has a national-level industry award, such as romance, science fiction, mystery, or journalism, display that achievement as a hook to differentiate your book from the masses. Some of those top accolades include the Man Booker Prize, PEN Award, Christy

Award, Hugo Award, etc.

The purpose of displaying accolades is to differentiate your book from the huge inventory of titles on Amazon's website. Accolades act like marketing hooks that cause shoppers to stop, take notice, and give your book stronger consideration. As I stated earlier, if you've got 'em, flaunt 'em.

However, I realize that many authors reading this book may not have a bestseller award, a sales milestone, or a major endorsement to display. That's okay. Most books don't have these items. That's why it's so important to create an effective marketing hook using language that I described in Chapter 1.

But, even if you're just getting started in your author career and don't have the fancy awards listed above, there are still options at your disposal. Read on for three ideas.

What If You Don't Have Any Accolades?

Before we move forward, let's talk about the other side of accolades. What if you don't have any? That's a fair question. Aside from celebrities who are already famous, the average first-time starts out with no awards and no track record.

For example, when you saw the accolades for *The Girl on the Train,* did you think, "That is a bestselling book from a well-known author. I can't match that success. How do I create a persuasive Amazon page when I'm just beginning my career?" Actually, there are steps you can take within your control to generate legitimate accolades for yourself. Let's look at three options:

1. Display "Over 100 positive reviews"

The amount of positive reviews your book receives on Amazon represents influential marketing language. Many Amazon shoppers judge books based on the amount of positive reviews from other readers. Therefore, once you receive at least 100 positive reviews, turn that achievement into an accolade featured at the top of your book detail page. Amazon defines any 5-star and 4-star review as positive. So, you can combine those two groups together into one total number.

By the way, if you are struggling or confused about getting more Amazon reviews, see my book, *The Author's Guide to Marketing Books on Amazon*. In Chapter 2, I explain four ways to get more Amazon customer reviews for free.

Even if you're early in your author career, it's quite feasible to get 100 positive reviews that commend your book. Once you reach that mark, add that achievement to your book detail page. Then, keep it updated. As you get 250, 500, or even 1,000 positive reviews, continue to display the number for people to see. Let that phrase act like social proof to convince new readers their peers have given your book a glowing recommendation.

2. Display local or regional awards

Persuasive language can also include any local or regional book awards that you might have received. You may not have hit a major bestseller list. But, almost every area of the country offers regional literary contests and book awards. Most contests are free to enter or charge an inexpensive fee.

Do a little research on Google and search for local contests where your book would qualify. You don't have to win the contest. Even if you get nominated within a specific category, add that mention to the top of your book detail page. For example, you could display, "Winner of the Southeast Regional Book Award" or "Nominated for Best New Fiction of the Northwest Award."

3. List endorsements from notable leaders

When it comes to marketing language, nothing you say about your book will ever be as powerful as what other people say about your book. People tend to trust the opinion of a peer more than the marketing text from an advertisement. That's why you see so many books displaying endorsements from notable leaders.

Examples of persuasive endorsements can be a recommendation from a well-known author who writes similar books in your genre. Or, it could be a testimonial from a well-known business executive, athlete, minister, musician, politician, etc. If you personally know anyone famous, send them a free copy of your book and ask if they would provide you with an endorsement.

When you receive an endorsement, take full advantage of displaying that praise on your book's Amazon page.

If you don't know anyone famous, you probably have a friend who knows someone famous. Ask your friend if they would make an introduction or pass along your book and facilitate an endorsement.

Also, the next chapter will explain how to secure endorsements for your book. You will find Chapter 6 helpful if you are struggling to get endorsements or need a pep talk to get motivated in that area.

You may not yet have the accolades of a bestselling author, but you can still add persuasive elements to your book description. Don't fall prey to comparing yourself to the big shots and get depressed. Improve your book description with the three elements just described that are within your means. Any author can win more readers by displaying the fact of receiving lots of positive reviews, local awards, or endorsements.

Otherwise, when it comes to accolades...

If you've got 'em, flaunt 'em.

6

HOW TO GET ENDORSEMENTS THAT SELL BOOKS

The theme of this book is that language powers the book sale. When people see persuasive hooks and book descriptions, their decision-making process is swayed. As an author, you have the control to create book hooks, titles, value statements, and book descriptions that influence people's desire to buy.

However, there is another facet of language that exceeds all of these elements, the language of other people recommending your book. Read this next sentence carefully:

No matter what marketing text you create for your book, nothing will ever be as powerful as other people praising your book.

This truth is incredibly important. The language of other people praising your book is superior to any marketing language you could create. For example, in the previous chapter, I showed the power of Bill Gates endorsing the book, *Factfulness*. His testimonial creates a lot of book sales by sheer dent of his name showing up.

Why is the praise of other people so valuable for your book? People trust what their peers say much more than they trust what you say. The opinions from peers matter more than the marketing copy for your book. This principle explains why you see so many books with endorsements from notable leaders on the front cover or on the book's Amazon page.

If getting endorsements from other people is so important, you might wonder why I'm sharing this information near the end of the book. I'm explaining this topic now because it's the one part of marketing language that you *cannot* completely control. You can always ask people to endorse your book, but you cannot control their response. Some people you ask will say yes. Others will turn you down or ignore your request.

Therefore, I advocate that you work first on the elements of language that you can control as described in Chapters 1 – 5. As you get comfortable implementing those tactics, then pursue endorsements with all of your might. This chapter will provide you with shortcuts to increase the odds of a positive response. Keep this principle in mind. When readers see an endorsement for a book, this aspect usually applies:

People care more about WHO says the endorsement.
People care less about WHAT is said in the endorsement.

"Who" is more important than "what." In other words, you could receive the most glowing book endorsement in the world. But, if the comment comes from someone whom people don't know, then that endorsement means nothing. It's like water rolling off a duck's back.

Therefore, the only endorsements that matter are from people who are famous, esteemed, or have a high profile.

I'm serious. It is a waste of time to seek endorsements from individuals that people would not recognize or respect. It's wiser to focus your energies on getting one or two high-profile endorsers, than spending time getting lots of endorsements from people who the masses wouldn't admire.

Seek endorsements from people who are genuine influencers. The Cambridge Dictionary defines an influencer as:

Someone who affects or changes the way that other people behave.

A true influencer has the ability to persuade a lot of people to buy your book simply by telling people that they like it. They represent the ultimate form of "word of mouth." If you receive an endorsement from this type of individual, their fans will buy your book without thinking twice.

In today's culture, an influencer is someone with a huge following who can spur hundreds, if not thousands, of sales by sheer dent of making a positive recommendation. You want endorsements from real influencers, rather than people that no one has ever heard of.

If you only get endorsements from people who are obscure or unknown, their comments can actually work against you. If readers see a list of unknown endorsers for your book, they can surmise, "Your book must not be very good, because I've never heard of the people who gave you a testimonial."

I'm not saying that an endorsement has to be from someone who everyone would know, such as Oprah or Stephen Colbert. For an endorsement to be effective, it needs to be from someone who you target audience would recognize. Thus, it could be someone that I would find obscure, but whom the readers in your genre would respect.

To be clear, endorsements for your book are different from the customer reviews that people leave on Amazon's website. You definitely want a lot of Amazon reviews. Those reviews act as social proof that many people are reading your book. Readers look at the number of Amazon reviews your book has to see if it is considered popular. But, when they look at endorsements, they care more about who said it.

Examples of genuine influencers worth pursuing include:

- Well-known authors who write similar books in your genre
- Social media personalities or tastemakers with lots of followers
- Pastors of a large church or directors of a ministry or non-profit

- Professional athletes or musicians with noted success
- Industry experts, professors, or noted educators
- Politicians who appeal to a wide audience

Logically speaking, these types of people typically fall into one of two categories:

1. Influencers you know

2. Influencers you don't know

Obviously, the latter category is much bigger. But, it's always wise to start with influencers you may know in order to build momentum and boost your confidence level. First, let's look at how to request endorsements from influencers you do know.

How to Request Endorsements from Influencers You Know

Step 1 – Identify realistic influencer candidates

I always recommend that you start with "low-hanging fruit" to build your confidence requesting endorsements. It's much easier to ask someone for a testimonial when you already have a personal relationship. Asking for a favor is usually an easy request. Once you get one high-profile endorsement, use that momentum to contact other candidates you know and say, "So-and-so has already endorsed my book, so you can feel comfortable doing it as well."

If you barely know someone or haven't spoken in over a

year, save those people for the next section, "How to request endorsements from people you don't know."

Step 2 – Use a script to make your request professional

Before you send an email request or call an influencer you know to ask for an endorsement, put together language that sounds polite, confident, and convincing. Feel free to use my script below to send someone you know an email request or leave a phone message:

Hi ___,

I hope you are well. (The next sentence is optional) The last time we spoke, we discussed [Insert topic of your previous conversation or a compliment about that individual.]

I'm excited to let you know that I'm publishing a new book called, [Insert Title.] The book is set to release on [Insert publication date]. My book is about [Insert your marketing hook here]. Readers will enjoy this book because [Insert one or two value statements here].

Since you are admired by many of the readers who I hope buy my book, your endorsement would be incredibly helpful. Would you be open to providing a brief testimonial about my book, even just one or two sentences?

(This part is optional) I have already received endorsements from other highly regarded individuals like you, including [Insert names of other similar endorsers].

If it would save you time, I'm happy to provide some basic language for a testimonial that you could easily adapt or revise and send back to me.

Your endorsement would really mean a lot, and I'd be happy to return the favor in the future. Reply to this email and I'll send you a copy of my manuscript to review. Or, you are welcome to call me at [Insert phone number] to discuss the details.

Sincerely, _____

Step 3 – If an influencer candidate declines your offer

Influencers are human, so treat them the same way you'd like to be treated. If someone declines your endorsement request, politely thank him or her for taking time to respond. Then, leave them alone. Never beg, cajole, or act desperate for an endorsement.

Take a long-term view and respect the relationship so that you can potentially ask again in the future. Just say, "No problem. I appreciate your willingness to consider my request. Let me know if there is anything I can do for you." However, if you know the person well, always ask for a referral to another influencer whom they may know. That follow-up question could open the door to several new opportunities.

Step 4 – If an influencer agrees to endorse your book

If an influencer agrees to endorse your book, do a little happy dance. Then, thank that person, send them a copy of your manuscript, and tell them the deadline for when you need to receive their testimonial. Since influencers are typically quite busy, they may need a few weeks to review your book and send you their written thoughts. So, be sure to give people plenty of advance notice.

When you reply to an agreeable influencer, you can "grease the skids" for faster response by including samples of other endorsements you might have received. That way, the new influencers can get a flavor for what to say about your book.

Also, here's an inside industry secret. Did you know that many of the testimonials you see on bestselling books were not written by the endorser? Instead, the author, literary agent, or publisher wrote them. Then, those blurbs were sent to the endorser for final approval. Most influencers are so busy that they don't have time to write an endorsement. But, they are happy to approve a positive testimonial that is written to sound like them. Be prepared to take similar action with busy influencers whom you contact.

How to Request Endorsements from Influencers You Don't Know

Obviously, there are more people that you don't know that people you do know. Plus, most authors have a fantasy list of endorsers they'd love to get, such as Oprah, Bill Gates, or the President of the United States. Good luck.

However, you can take steps to identify realistic candidates whom you don't know and reach out to see if they would be comfortable endorsing your book.

Step 1A – Identify a friend, co-worker, or relative who knows someone famous.

This is the easiest and quickest path to success. Ask your friend, co-worker, or relative to make an introduction for you. If the introduction is successful, then provide the famous person with a copy of your book and use my script in the previous section to complete your request.

Step 1B – If you do not know someone who could make an introduction, then list the likely endorsement candidates whom you'd like to contact and got to Step 2.

Step 2 – If your influencer candidate has written a book (and most have), read a copy and post a positive review on your author blog or social media pages.

Take the lead by doing that person a favor first. Give their book a glowing review on your blog or social media pages. If you post the review on social media, tag the influencer's name in your book review so that he or she can see the action you took to help them.

Step 3 – Visit the influencer's website and locate their email address or contact form.

Send the influencer a message that says, "I really liked your book, and then ask a simple, open-ended question to start a friendly dialogue." For example, you could ask:

- *How did you come up with that clever idea in Chapter 3?*
- *What was the hardest part about writing your book?*
- *Who designed your website or book cover?*

Step 4A – If the influencer doesn't respond, let them go and move on to another influencer on your list.

Or, if you are feeling bold, send a follow-up question and ask for a referral to another influencer whom they know. It may be a long shot, but it's possible.

Step 4B – If the influencer responds, do not immediately ask for an endorsement. Take time to reply and continue the dialogue. Build the relationship and think long term.

If you have something of value the influencer would appreciate, such as a helpful article or an interesting website link, forward it to them.

Your goal is to get the influencer to respond to two or three follow-up messages over time. That helps increase their comfort level with you. As you sense their comfort level increase, then you can politely ask for an endorsement. Use the script from the previous section to make your request.

Step 5 – Whether or not an influencer provides an endorsement, always ask that individual for referrals to other influencers.

Most legitimate influencers are part of a network and know several other people just like them. Asking an influencer for referrals can be a gold mine of new opportunity.

Step 6 – If an influencer mentions or recommends other people to contact, reach out to those individuals with a message starting with, "Hi, Influencer X encouraged me to contact you..." Then, repeat steps 1 – 5.

When I began my author career in 2002, I was 34 years old with a tiny database of contacts and no connections to anyone famous. But, I had a passion for my book. I truly believed it could help people. I channeled this belief into reaching out to industry leaders via email and setting up meetings at conferences. To my surprise, I was shocked by how many nice endorsements I received simply by making the request. The key to my success was having the courage to ask.

Likewise, do you have the courage to ask real influencers to endorse your book? There is nothing you can say as powerful than what an influencer says about your book. But, an influencer will never endorse your book unless you believe in yourself enough to ask.

If language is the power of the sale, then influencers are the wizards of language.

Woo them wisely. They can help your book sales spread like wildfire!

7

AMAZON'S SECRET MARKETING BACK DOOR

In this chapter, I've saved the best for last! Earlier in the book, I told you that a special secret was coming. Now that we're here, I'm going to put myself in the marketing hot seat. How's this for a hook?

- What if you could ensure Amazon shoppers always see your best marketing text?
- What if you could improve your book's marketing copy whenever you desire for free?
- What if you could override your publisher and improve Amazon's marketing text yourself?

Here's a little secret. You are never stuck with bad marketing text on Amazon. It's possible to change your book's marketing copy on their website any time you desire.

Amazon's website has a "back door" that lets any author upload new promotional text for their books. This "back door" is available to every author, regardless if you are traditionally-published or self-published.

Why does Amazon's back door matter? If you're a traditionally-published author or worked with a third-party self-publishing outfit, you may have cringed to see outdated or bland marketing text sitting on your book's Amazon page. You may think there is no way to improve it. That concern comes from the reality that most publishing houses are too busy, too short-staffed, or too inexperienced to update their books on Amazon – let alone craft top-notch promotional copy in the first place.

Plus, if your book goes on to win an award or get a new endorsement, good luck getting it added to your book detail page on Amazon. Publishing companies are notorious for launching new books and never updating the success of their backlist titles.

This chapter will walk you through the steps to use Amazon's clever back door by yourself. My goal is to help you take more control over the way your book appears to shoppers on Amazon. If people see your book displayed with compelling marketing copy, you will naturally sell more books. Your publisher will benefit as well, so they'll appreciate you doing them a favor.

3 Reasons to Use Amazon's Back Door

Here are three reasons why you should take advantage of Amazon's secret back door:

1. Your book's marketing text has a direct influence on your book sales.

As I explained in Chapter 1, language is the power of the book sale. When people look at your book on Amazon, the marketing copy they see will either help persuade or dissuade them from making a purchase. For example, remember those shocking statistics about Amazon from the start of Chapter 5? Their domination is overwhelming. But, if you've got excellent marketing copy, it will help encourage people to buy your book. If your marketing copy is boring, that text can work against you and hinder sales.

2. Different versions of your book need the same marketing text.

In most cases, your book has more than one version on Amazon's website. For instance, your book might have been originally published in hardcover. Then, the paperback version was introduced. Almost every book has an e-book version. And, many books are now converted into audio versions. That's four different versions of the same book on Amazon. People will consider buying all four types based on their reading preferences.

Here's the problem. Each version of your book has a completely different webpage on Amazon's site. And, the marketing text doesn't remain the same unless you check it before adding that version of your book to the website. Most authors and publishers fail to crosscheck and keep a book's marketing text consistent.

Look for yourself. Go on Amazon and you'll find thousands

of books (maybe yours) that have radically different marketing copy from one version to another. This discrepancy prevents the most compelling text from being seen by anyone who views your books. You never know which version will be a reader's first impression of your work. First impressions do matter. Therefore, you want every version of your book to have the same excellent marketing text that is updated and as persuasive as possible.

3. Poor formatting can cost you book sales.

Let's try a little experiment. At the time of this writing, the text below is the actual marketing copy pulled from Amazon's website for a book entitled, *Boundaries in Marriage*. When you see this huge amount of words smashed into one giant paragraph, do you feel enticed to read it?

Learn when to say yes and when to say no--to your spouse and to others--to make the most of your marriage. Only when a husband and wife know and respect each other's needs, choices, and freedom can they give themselves freely and lovingly to one another. Boundaries are the "property lines" that define and protect husbands and wives as individuals. Once they are in place, a good marriage can become better, and a less-than-satisfying one can even be saved. Drs. Henry Cloud and John Townsend, counselors and authors of the award-winning bestseller Boundaries, show couples how to apply the 10 laws of boundaries that can make a real difference in relationships. They help husbands and wives understand the friction points or serious hurts and betrayals in their marriage—and move beyond them to the mutual care, respect, affirmation, and intimacy they both long for. Boundaries in Marriage helps couples: • Set and main-

tain personal boundaries and respect those of their spouse•
Establish values that form a godly structure and architecture for
their marriage• Protect their marriage from different kinds of
"intruders"• Work with a spouse who understands and values
boundaries—or work with one who doesn't.

If you're like me, you felt no desire to read that huge paragraph. It just looks like a big blob of words with no appeal
whatsoever. You probably just skipped reading it altogether
and jumped to this paragraph.

Imagine how Amazon shoppers feel when they see a huge
chunk of words. Based on the unappealing text formatting,
very few people would take time to read the description for
Boundaries in Marriage unless the book was personally
recommended via word of mouth or they are someone
desperate to fix their marriage. Yet, most shoppers aren't in
that position. Most shoppers on Amazon's website are
browsing without any word of mouth recommendation, nor
do they feel any relational desperation.

But, wait...there's more. If you view the Kindle e-book
version of *Boundaries in Marriage* on Amazon, you will see
completely different marketing text. It's another big paragraph that is equally frustrating to read. Yet, it says something completely different from the marketing text on the
paperback format. There is no consistency between the
versions of the same book on Amazon's website.

Why does this problem matter? This discrepancy prevents
shoppers from seeing the best marketing text to influence
their decision to buy. It's like shooting yourself in the foot
for no good reason.

If you want to sell books to the masses, you must display persuasive marketing copy that the masses can easily read and appreciate. Bad formatting causes people to ignore your book and label it as unprofessional. Any of the issues listed below could hinder your book sales if they appear on your book's page on Amazon's website:

- Marketing text that is boring and lacks emotional persuasion
- Marketing copy smashed together into one huge paragraph
- Lack of putting statements or points into easy-to-read bulleted lists
- No persuasive book hook at the beginning of marketing text
- Lack of displaying persuasive testimonials, endorsements, and awards
- Inconsistent marketing text across various formats of the same book
- Displaying too much marketing text that is overkill rather than concise

Fortunately, Amazon provides a way for any author to fix these problems whenever needed – for FREE. By now, you're waiting with baited breath to know the secret, "Okay, Rob, how do I access Amazon's back door?" The answer lies inside your Amazon Author Central account.

How to Access the Amazon "Back Door"

The Amazon Author Central account provides any author

with the ability to change a book's marketing copy whenever desired. If you're not familiar with setting up your Author Central account, see Chapter 3 in my book, *The Author's Guide to Marketing Books on Amazon.* Setting up an account is free and only takes a few simple steps. I won't bore you with the details here. You can always reference Amazon's website for tutorials or contact their author support team for help.

In this section, I'll walk you through 10 easy steps to access your books and make desired changes to the marketing text:

Step 1 – Log in to your free account at:

https://authorcentral.amazon.com/

Step 2 – Once inside your account, click on the word at the top that says, "Books."

Step 3 – When you click on "Books," it brings up a new screen with all of the books you've added to your author account.

Step 4 – Choose the book that you want to update the marketing copy. You can click on the title or book cover image displayed to make your selection.

Step 5 – After you select a book, a new webpage will appear that shows all of the details about your book. Scroll down the page and click on the tab that says, "Editorial Reviews."

Step 6 – Under the "Editorial Reviews" tab, scroll down until you see a section labeled, "Product Description." In that section, the marketing copy for your book is displayed.

Step 7 – In most cases, there will be a small button that says "Edit" next to your book's product description. Click on the "Edit" button.

Note: If you don't see an "Edit" button next to your book's product description, there might be a link that says, "Request a correction." Click on that link to contact Amazon's Author Central customer service team for help. You can send them the updated marketing copy to install for you. Or, you can ask them to reinstall the "Edit" button for your book.

Step 8 – After clicking on the "Edit" button, a new window will pop up on your computer screen that lets you type or paste new marketing copy for your book. Amazon recommends using a plain text editor like Notepad to paste in new text. Rich text editors, such as Microsoft Word, can cause formatting issues which delay or prevent your update from being processing.

Step 9 – Type or paste the new marketing copy for your book into Amazon's editing window using bolded font, italics, and bulleted lists as needed. Then, click on the "Preview" button at the bottom right corner to see how the changes look before sending them to Amazon.

Step 10 – Once everything looks good to you in the preview window, click on the "Save changes" button to submit the changes to Amazon. Those changes will usually appear on your book's Amazon page within 24 – 48 hours. Now you're in control of your book's success!

To review Amazon's specific guidelines for updating the marketing text for your book, click on this link:

https://amzn.to/KqMoLa

Important Note:

Be sure to update the marketing text for every version of the same book. You can find the different versions listed for each book by going to your book's specific page as mentioned in Step 5 earlier. In the top right corner of every book page, there is a box that says, "Editions," which displays all of a book's editions for sale on Amazon's website. Editions can include hard cover, paperback, e-book, and audio formats. Each edition listed is a hyperlink you can click to access that version's details and make any desired updates.

Besides changing your book's marketing text, you can also use the sections listed under the "Editorial Reviews" screen to add new endorsements, industry reviews, or insert your author bio. This is a great way to keep your book updated with the most relevant details and testimonials from influential people.

Now that you know how to access Amazon's secret back door, use it wisely. As a reminder, always lead with your strongest marketing text. For instance, if your book has hit a major bestseller list, show that information first. If you received an endorsement from a famous person or well-known media organization, show that testimonial at the top of your marketing text as well. Otherwise, put the marketing hook for your book at the top of your product description text. Use a bolded font to make all of the words stand out on the page.

~

Amazon's "back door" enables authors to regain control over marketing their books at the world's largest online retailer. You don't have to beg or wait for your publisher to fix the marketing copy. You have the power to change your book's text at anytime for every book you've written and for every version of that book.

If you're an indie author who wants to keep your books competitive in the marketplace, you're on a level playing field. You can make the same improvements at any time. It's a big step forward for author empowerment.

Use Amazon's back door to upgrade the words that shoppers see when viewing your books on Amazon. Better marketing copy equals better book sales. The power to display persuasive promotional text is now fully in your hands.

CONCLUSION

We live in a modern era. But, modern technology just transmits your marketing language to more people. If your marketing text is compelling, more people will be influenced by the words you write. If your marketing text is dull, more people will lose interest by your lackluster words. I wrote this book to help you avoid the latter fate.

However, before you show your marketing language to the public, there is one very important individual you must convince first. That person is you. You have more influence over the success of your marketing text than anyone else. But, in order to generate that success, you must believe that your book is worth investing the required time and energy. Other people are less likely to feel excited about your book unless you feel excited. Therefore, never forget this principle:

The first book sale is always to yourself.

Okay, the first sale may be to your mom, but you get my point. You are always the first customer for your book. You must be impressed and excited by what you've written. You must feel confident that people will enjoy the entertainment, education, or inspiration within your manuscript.

If you do not feel this enthusiasm, that's okay. Be honest. Then, ask yourself if you're willing to take the necessary steps to raise your enthusiasm, such as recruiting beta readers for constructive feedback, hiring a professional editor, or honing your writing skills. These steps will work to solidify your confidence. When you put in the work for success, you earn the right to feel confident about your book.

As you finish reading this guide, I'd like to close with a personal question:

Do you truly believe in your book?

I don't mean to pry or overstep my place in the matter. But, the belief you feel towards your book will determine your willingness to apply the advice that I've provided. A belief in your own book is critical to write the essential marketing language described in the previous chapters. Without a steadfast belief that your book is good, you will burn out when the work gets difficult. So, may I ask you again...

Do you truly believe in your book?

When you can eagerly say yes, then you have what it takes to get other people to believe in your book. And, when you get other people to believe in your book, you gain access to most powerful marketing language in the world: word of mouth.

However, this transcendent language rarely occurs by itself. You must plant the seeds and nurture them in order for word of mouth to grow. Those seeds comprise the six areas of convincing language covered earlier in this book:

1. Develop enticing marketing hooks

2. Create a compelling book title

3. Explain the value of your book

4. Write a persuasive book description

5. Display any accolades

6. Get other people to endorse your book

The power to create dynamic marketing text is within your control. I hope you will grab that control and enjoy wielding the power of words.

I am honored that you chose me and this guide to be a part of your author journey. I wish you all the best to your career and your book sales!

Sincerely,

Rob Eagar

Wildfire Marketing

MAKE AN AUTHOR HAPPY TODAY

If you found the material in this book helpful, I'd be grateful if you took a few minutes to write a review on Amazon.

When you post a review, it makes a huge difference to help new readers find my books.

Your review would make my day!

Thank you,

Rob

MY FREE GIFT FOR YOU

Get three e-books to help jumpstart your book sales for FREE:

Find Readers and Sell Books on a Shoestring Budget

Mastering Book Hooks for Authors

The Ultimate Book Marketing Plan Template for Authors

Join my email newsletter and get these three e-books. Each e-book can be downloaded as a file to your computer or added to any e-reader device. You will also receive my weekly e-newsletter packed with expert marketing advice for authors.

Download these three e-books for free today at:

https://www.startawildfire.com/free-ebooks-ag

ABOUT ROB EAGAR

Rob Eagar is a marketing consultant and one of the most accomplished book marketing experts in America. He has coached over 450 authors, advised top publishing houses, provided industry intelligence, and created instructional resources for writers. Highlights from Rob's consulting work with clients include:

- Helped books hit the *New York Times* bestseller lists three different ways
- Built and expanded email lists by over 25,000 subscribers in nine months
- Rebranded multiple authors who became *New York Times* bestsellers
- Designed numerous author websites that doubled visitor traffic within 60 days
- Developed bestselling book titles, marketing hooks, and book descriptions
- Revived a backlist book to hit *New York Times* bestseller list after 23 years in print

Rob founded Wildfire Marketing, a consulting practice that has attracted numerous bestselling authors, including Dr. Gary Chapman, DeVon Franklin, Lysa TerKeurst, Wanda Brunstetter, Harville Hendrix, and Dr. John Townsend. In addition, he's consulted with imprints of the world's best-known publishers, such as HarperCollins (Thomas Nelson, Zondervan), Hachette (FaithWords), Simon & Schuster

(Howard Books) and numerous small to mid-sized publishers.

Rob's expertise stems from starting out as a successful multi-published author. In 2002, he self-published his first book and generated a consistent six-figure income, long before the rise of social media and Amazon. His book was later purchased by a traditional publisher, sold over 50,000 copies, and remained on bookstore shelves for over 10 years.

His success attracted the attention of other authors who sought out Rob for marketing advice. This led him to found Wildfire Marketing in 2007 and provide marketing education to authors around the world. In addition, Rob partnered with Writer's Digest to publish the book, *Sell Your Book Like Wildfire*, and teach his online video course, *Mastering Amazon for Authors*.

Rob's industry-leading instruction can now be found in *The Author's Guide* series, a collection of books dedicated to teaching critical marketing topics, including:

The Author's Guide to Marketing Books on Amazon

The Author's Guide to Write Text That Sells Books

The Author's Guide to Email Marketing

Rob has served as a contributing writer and educator for Book Business Magazine, Digital Book World, Writer's Digest, and Reedsy. His national media appearances include interviews on the CBS Early Show, CNN Radio, and the *Los Angeles Times*. His background includes a marketing degree from Auburn University and 10 years of corporate sales experience before working full-time in publishing.

Rob is married to Ashley the Wonderful. When he isn't consulting, you can find Rob fly-fishing for monster trout, breaking 40mph on his road bike, or loudly playing his drums. Ashley would prefer that he join her to quietly paint, work in their garden, or watch Jane Austen movies. They reside near Atlanta, Georgia. For more details about Rob, his books, and his consulting services, visit his website at:

http://www.RobEagar.com

GET EXPERT HELP FOR YOUR BOOKS

Are you're tired of trying to figure out book marketing by yourself? What if an experienced coach guided you to the next level? Get personal help from one of the most accomplished experts in America:

Book Marketing Master Class

You can master your book sales. It's not a dream. The Book Marketing Master Class teaches how to master all key aspects of marketing a book. Whether you're a first-time author or a seasoned bestseller, Rob Eagar will show you how to:

- Attract more readers using the power of free content and email.
- Create persuasive language, including hooks, titles, and back cover copy.
- Construct a complete marketing plan to maximize the book launch sequence.
- Turn your author website into a sales machine.
- Maximize advertising on Amazon and Facebook.
- Connect with online influencers and turn media interviews into book sales.
- Discover multiple ways to create new income from your book content.

Rob's expertise applies to fiction and non-fiction, first-timer or bestseller, indie author or traditionally-published. He will personally teach you his proven marketing techniques and apply his instruction to your specific books, goals, and experience level. Work with Rob in person or receive instruction via live video sessions. Include your team and get everyone coached up at the same time. Receive follow-up access to ask Rob questions, hold you accountable, and request his review of your work. For details, visit:

https://www.startawildfire.com/consulting/book-marketing-master-class

Personal 90-Minute
Author Coaching Sessions

Are your book sales stagnant? Got a nagging marketing or publishing question? Ready to raise the bar on your author career? Reach your goals by talking directly with a world-class expert. Schedule a personal 90-minute author coaching session with Rob Eagar.

Individual coaching sessions include direct access to Rob to ask questions and learn how to improve your book marketing skills. Using live video screenshare technology, he will walk you step-by-step through everything you need to know. Get immediate answers to reach more readers, build a larger audience, sell more books, and increase your author revenue. For details about purchasing a 90-minute Author Coaching Session, visit:

https://www.startawildfire.com/consulting/author-consultation

OTHER BOOKS BY ROB EAGAR

The Author's Guide to Marketing Books on Amazon

The Author's Guide to Email Marketing

For more information, visit:

http://www.RobEagar.com

Made in United States
North Haven, CT
24 May 2024

52903498R00089